SCHOOLS COUNCIL WORKING PAPER 63

Curricular needs
of slow learners

report of the Schools Council
Curricular Needs of Slow-learning
Pupils Project

W. K. BRENNAN

Evans/Methuen Educational

Foreword

The Schools Council Curricular Needs of Slow-learning Pupils Project (1971–74) was set up on the recommendation of the Council's Working Party on Special Education. Directed by W. K. Brennan, Inspector for Special Education, Inner London Education Authority, and later Assistant Education Officer for Special Education, ILEA, this was the first project in the Council's programme of work in special education. Its aims were to study good practice in a wide variety of schools (primary, secondary and special) and to describe the best of existing practice. The project was concerned with the whole curriculum for the academically least successful 15–20 per cent of the school population between the ages of 5 and 16.

The project team visited 502 primary, secondary and special schools throughout England and Wales, observing and analysing good practice in a variety of organizational contexts and across all subject areas, revisiting 152 of these schools in the final year of the project. They addressed over a hundred teachers' groups, and participated in a number of national and local courses, supporting, through the Cambridge Institute of Education, a series of two-day courses for teachers of slow learners arranged by area training organizations. Mr Brennan also acted as consultant to the Inner London Education Authority Television Service in the production of a series of ten videotapes, *Teaching the Slow Learner*, using schools involved in the project.

Although the author is an officer of the Inner London Education Authority, this report reflects the views of the project and not necessarily those of the ILEA.

The other publication from the project, also by W. K. Brennan, is a practical teacher's guide on the reading development of pupils with learning difficulties, published in 1978 as Schools Council Curriculum Bulletin 7, *Reading for Slow Learners: a Curriculum Guide*.

Acknowledgements

Very special thanks are due to the local education authorities which allowed the project to have access to their schools. In the schools, headteachers and teaching staff welcomed members of the project team and gave freely of their time and experience in a totally unselfish manner. Without their assistance and stimulation this work would not have been possible. The staffs of the Schools Council and the Cambridge Institute of Education were a continuous source of support and encouragement, as were the members of the project Consultative Committee. Thanks are also due to the many teacher colleagues and others who made written submissions to the project or engaged its members in lively discussion.

The project team acknowledge Essex Education Committee for office accommodation and computer assistance; the headmaster and staff of Trinity Primary School, Chelmsford, for their friendly acceptance and support of the project team; the Inner London Education Authority for secondment of the project director, and the Essex and Wolverhampton Education Committees for secondment of the project research associates.

Preface

This book is based upon three years of work in primary, secondary and special schools in England and Wales. It discusses those aspects of the full report of the Schools Council project on the curricular needs of slow-learning pupils which should be of value to teachers responsible for slow learners in the schools. Inspectors, advisers, educational psychologists and other professional workers who support the teachers should also find much of value. But it is hoped that the book will, in addition, be of interest to parents of slow learners, school governors and managers, members of education committees and other concerned members of the public, because the curriculum offered to slow learners is regarded as being of concern to the whole community, and teachers need the support of these partners if there is to be improvement in the quality of education.

In some respects this book is a tentative offering. The project had a large task and a small team; depth of study was consequently limited; and judgements frequently rested on the experience of individuals. Nor are the judgements absolute: they are made in the framework of the strengths and weaknesses observed in the schools and are, at best, comparative. Nevertheless, an attempt is made to be positive, to acknowledge strengths where they exist, to define and criticize weaknesses and to suggest ways forward to improved education for slow learners. In doing this it was necessary to develop a background from a review of curriculum literature (Chapter III) and also to discuss the general background against which teachers of slow learners perform their task (Chapter IV) and the schools in which they work (Chapter II).

Readers should make special note that it was the *curriculum* for slow learners which was studied in the project. Curriculum is *not* the same as teaching. This is important. Judgements made in this book are mainly about curriculum and should not be generalized as referring to teaching standards. It is possible for good teaching to be conducted in poor curricula, or even in the absence of any curricula, and both situations were observed in project schools. Conversely, good curricula may fail to achieve objectives because of ineffective or inappropriate teaching, and this too was observed. To be highly effective, of course, education requires a combination of good curriculum with good teaching: this situation was rare in the project schools. This was not due to lack of teaching skill, for teaching skill was impressive overall; nor was it due to lack of care and concern for the welfare of slow learners in the schools. The fact is that much more thought and attention has been given to these aspects of work with slow learners than has been given to curriculum construction and development. There are acceptable reasons for this situation set out in Chapter IV, but the situation must not be allowed to continue.

If the curriculum for slow learners is to be improved, and through it the quality of their education, then there must be much more attention to curriculum. The argument in this book is that the responsibility for bringing about these improvements is in the schools, where responsibility for the curriculum should remain. Part of the argument is that the schools need more support in carrying out their task and that local education authorities should accept more responsibility for providing the support within better organized arrangements for continuous curriculum review and development. Parents and members of the community must also play their part. They must renounce the luxury of criticism from the sidelines and be prepared to make their contribution to curricular improvement. Anything less than such all-round effort is unlikely to be successful. Whether or not the proposals made in this book are adopted is unimportant. What is important is that they should stimulate thought, discussion and action which has the same objective of improvement in the education of slow learners.

I. The background of the project

The brief for the project defined the slow learners as: the 15 to 20 per cent of pupils making least satisfactory progress in their school work. Or, to define them in a different way, the slow learners are the pupils who are unable to manage learning tasks which are successfully completed by 75 to 80 per cent of their age peers. These less able pupils were to be found in the infant, junior, secondary and special schools of England and Wales, the majority of them within the ordinary schools.

On the curriculum, the brief was exceptionally broad. The importance of achievement in basic subjects was stressed, while noting the danger that a prescribed minimum could become a ceiling. Dangers inherent in utilitarian approaches to the curriculum were also noted and a balance suggested which included the development of concepts, the stimulation of curiosity and imagination, and the education of the emotions. Social education was accorded importance and related to vocational competence as well as to homemaking and family-life skills.

At this point the project team was assembled together with the project's consultative committee, consisting of representatives of Schools Council committees, experienced teachers of slow learners, tutors of advanced courses in special education, headteachers and remedial advisers. Consistent with Schools Council policy, the majority of the committee members were teachers working in schools. They represented a formidable range of experience in education generally as well as with slow learners, covering all stages of the school system and drawn from widely differing parts of England and Wales. In matters of policy and principle the consultative committee was a valuable source of advice for the project director and his colleagues throughout the work, while equally valuable administrative support came from the staff of the Schools Council and the Cambridge Institute of Education, the latter the grant-holder for the project.

It was decided that the design of the project should allow for a broad examination of the curriculum for slow learners across all the stages of education throughout a large number of schools in England and Wales.

The decision was taken reluctantly as it involved the abandonment of any attempt to study aspects of the curriculum in depth and also made impossible any close study of the learning processes of the slow learners in the schools. Such studies would have restricted the project to very narrow areas of the curriculum as well as requiring arbitrary selection of such areas, and it was thought that the technical and personnel resources allocated to the project would have been hard pressed to sustain work of quality. The broad design was held to be more suited to the resources and the task of an initial survey. It would certainly allow a report based upon the known variety of provision for slow learners; it would allow the mapping of curricular activities and discussion of the comparative strengths and weaknesses within the observed curricula; and it would provide a basis for suggestions for sharpening, extending or improving curricula. By involving schools in many different areas, the project could reflect in its report the attitudes and opinions of a varied group of teachers of slow learners, factors which would be important in any attempts at subsequent curriculum development. Indeed, the most attractive feature of the selected design was the opportunity to establish a re-searched and rational base from which it would be possible to promote curriculum development projects related to knowledge about the existing pattern and quality in the education of slow-learning pupils.

In order to simplify the task of selecting schools for the project, and to give a firm base for project conclusions, the design required that the work of the project should be restricted to schools conducting successful curricula with slow learners. In this way descriptions of work in schools, collections of curricular materials from schools and any conclusions drawn from the work of the project would be put forward as representative, not of the whole range of curricular work with slow learners, but of the best of contemporary practice. It was a neat solution to many problems though it immediately raised the question about how success was to be judged and how communication with successful schools could be established. It was decided that success would be judged subjectively, by those who knew the schools well, and this decision indicated the first step in making contact with schools. Letters were sent to the chief education officers of all local education authorities in England and Wales inviting them to nominate to the project any of their schools judged to be conducting successful curricular work with slow-learning pupils. Similar letters went to colleges and departments of education, to tutors of advanced courses in special or remedial education, to the main professional associations for teachers, to the associations of teachers in special and remedial education, and to teachers' associations covering the main curriculum subjects, inviting them to nominate any school judged to be successful in work with slow-learning pupils. When schools were nominated from these latter sources, no approach was made by the project until permission had been obtained from the chief education officer of the appropriate local education authorities. It may be objected that not only was this procedure subjective but that it centred selection firmly on the LEA. Such an objection stands sustained, with the comment that the LEA is the institution closest to individual schools and there seemed no practical alternative which could generate a large sample of schools quickly enough for the project's needs. The procedure did have one safeguard. As nominations began to build up, some schools were nominated from more than one independent source and the principle of multiple nomination proved a useful 'sorter' in the early stages of the work.

The working design was deceptively simple for the complicated task which faced the project team. First, each project school was asked to complete a questionnaire on its background, curriculum and approach to the teaching of slow learners, and invited to submit documents on the curriculum. Project workers then made short introductory visits to the schools. From the information received, a master chart was prepared showing comparisons between each curriculum, school organization and teaching strengths. From the initial list of nominated schools, a smaller number of schools was selected for further detailed study. This smaller sample was chosen so as to be representative of all types of school and school organization, all types of curriculum organization and all areas of the curriculum, and the range of types of school environments and geographical spread were also taken into account. Second visits (by a different project worker) were paid to these schools, and the studies made at this stage were more positive and directed than those made initially.

It was never intended that the work of the project should be exclusively centred on the schools as institutions. Hence the design allowed for contact with teachers through their professional organizations and through teachers' centres, where attempts would be made to involve teachers in discussion groups. The major social, political and industrial groups known to have views on education were also invited to contribute comments based on experience of slow learners in the post-school world. In addition the careers officer of each LEA received a questionnaire and a request for comments. Finally there was a continuous survey of literature on curricula in general and curricula for slow learners.

Some idea of the activities generated by the project design can be derived from the following:

Visits to schools	810
Visits to further education colleges and school-leavers' centres/ courses	15
Meetings with groups of teachers	106
National conferences attended/contributed to	32
Contributions to area training organization/Department of Education and Science courses	20
Contributions to headteachers' conferences	5
Meetings of consultative committee	12
Visitors to the project	78
Inquiries processed by the project	200
Schools contacted	779
Questionnaires to participating schools	502
Questionnaires returned from schools and processed	438
Additional correspondence with schools (items)	1024
Questionnaires to careers officers	135
Questionnaires returned from careers officers and processed	119
Questionnaires to chief education officers	135
CEO questionnaires returned from assistant education officers for special education	98
Correspondence with teachers' associations, educational, political and social groups	214
Questionnaires and correspondence with teachers' centres	413
Detailed submissions of views from organized teachers' centre groups	80
Papers submitted by inspectors, headteachers and assistant teachers	54
Dissertations, articles and books surveyed	486
Items on curriculum from schools	732

II. The schools

The schools and the pupils

The 502 project schools were made up as follows: primary, 196; secondary, 183; special, 123. These schools were distributed over 135 local education authorities in England and Wales with over half of them situated in county or municipal boroughs, a third in urban districts and about one-fifth in rural districts (using the local government designations operating at the time of the survey). On average, one school in ten was situated in the older, inner-ring area of a city or large town. Most of the schools had been built since 1946, but 54 primary, 21 secondary and 22 special schools still occupied premises built before 1920. A split site or annexe featured in one school in five, and one in three of the primary and secondary schools, and one in six of the special schools, had temporary buildings.

The total roll of the schools was 220 431 pupils: 65 158 in primary, 141 842 in secondary and 13 431 in special schools. In the primary and secondary schools the overall ratio of boys to girls was 11:10 but the ratio increased to 14:10 in the special schools. Among slow learners in the ordinary schools the trend was unmistakably towards the special-school figure though the ratio could not be accurately calculated. Average rolls of schools were: primary, 332; secondary, 775; special, 109. Thus the primary- and secondary-school averages were higher than those for all schools at the time of the project (221 primary, 629 secondary); special schools were nearer to the national average (109 as against 107). It was not possible to calculate pupil–teacher ratios for slow learners in primary schools because of mixed-ability classes. However, the overall ratio in project primary schools was 28:1, against a national average of 29:1. Secondary-school ratios were calculated for identifiable, separate slow-learners' classes, giving a figure of 20:1, which may be compared with the overall national average of secondary schools of 19:1. The project special schools had a pupil–teacher ratio of 12:1 which exactly reflected the national average. Of course, these average figures conceal variations between individual schools, though the general picture they suggest is of project schools somewhat larger than average schools of the same type and with pupil–teacher ratios at about the national level.

There will undoubtedly be interest in the number of slow-learning pupils in the ordinary project schools. Here figures are necessarily subjective estimates based on information from the schools and observations on school visits, and averages again conceal variations between individual schools. As an average the 20 per cent suggested in the project brief appears far too pessimistic, and even the 15 per cent doubtful. A lowest estimate was 11 per cent, making a best estimate somewhere between that figure and the 15 per cent. Applied to the total pupil roll of project schools these percentages place the number of slow learners in those schools between 22 700 and 31 000.

It was not possible to study directly the social backgrounds of the slow learners in the schools. However, the situation disclosed by information from the schools suggested that the pupils were typical when measured against the existing experience of project workers. In home neighbourhoods, older working-class housing predominated followed closely by council housing. On average 60 per cent of homes were lacking in intellectual stimulus; 50 per cent lacked regular routine; 23 per cent were affected by poverty; and there was illness or disability in 18 per cent of the homes. Children from one-parent homes made up 13 per cent of the slow-learning pupils. Immigrant pupils formed 20 per cent of slow learners in primary schools, 28 per cent in secondary schools but only 11 per cent of special-school pupils. One explanation of this may be that the ordinary schools were selected as being successful with slow-learning pupils and this may have contributed to their ability to meet the needs of their immigrant pupils.

Teachers and supporting staff

The pupil–teacher ratios in the project schools were noted above; here other aspects of staffing are considered. In no school did the number of teachers with additional qualifications for work with slow learners amount to as many as half of the teaching staff. Such qualifications were most common in special schools (44 per cent), followed by secondary schools (28 per cent) and primary schools (4 per cent). Primary schools also trailed on head of department posts (27 per cent compared with secondary at 44 per cent); and on additional scale posts in slow-learner departments (8 per cent compared with secondary at 37 per cent). Special schools, in addition to headteachers, had deputy heads in 93 per cent of schools, senior teachers in 32 per cent of schools, and scale posts for a further 58 per cent of the schools.

School doctors, educational psychologists and school welfare workers were the most widely provided supporting staff, ranging around the 85–90 per cent level in all types of schools. Speech therapists worked in 80 per cent of primary and special schools but in only 28 per cent of secondary schools. Remedial advisory services supported 70 per cent of primary, 28 per cent of secondary and 21 per cent of special schools. Child guidance clinics had some contact with 75 per cent of all types of school. Most disappointing was the availability of special education inspectors or advisers for only 55 per cent of primary, 53 per cent of special and 43 per cent of secondary schools. Of course, as these schools are rated as successful in their LEAs, the inspectors and advisers may be spending their time where it is more needed! Direct involvement of social services department workers centred on the special schools and no doubt reflected the combinations of handicap and disadvantage found in those schools. Availability is one thing; adequacy of support is another. It has to be recorded here that, in the estimates of the schools, no supportive staff were rated more than 70 per cent adequate in any type of school, and differences between the schools did not appear to be significant.

Two categories of support for teachers are provided within schools. The first, the school counsellor, was significant only in secondary schools at 65 per cent availability and 33 per cent adequacy. The second, the nursery assistant, appeared in relation to slow learners in special schools only. On average there was a nursery assistant to every five teachers and, together with the teachers, this gave the special schools a pupil–adult ratio of 10:1.

School organization for slow learners

The way in which schools were organized for teaching slow learners fell into only two forms in primary and secondary schools – the separate special class and withdrawal from ordinary classes for special teaching. In primary schools 60 per cent had organized separate classes; in secondary schools, it was 62 per cent. Withdrawal teaching was organized in 78 per cent of primary and 54 per cent of secondary schools. Where both forms existed in the same school, separate classes were regarded as being for 'dull' pupils and withdrawal for those with more ability but with reading difficulties. Among the schools with separate classes for their slow learners, 12 per cent of primary and 50 per cent of secondary schools organized a separate class for each school year. This appeared to be the most satisfactory provision. Observation in the schools convinced project workers that the single special class in any type of school was rarely successful and usually took on the distressing features of a 'sink' class. A considered judgement was that the minimum was two special classes to cover the junior or secondary age-range. Where numbers did not allow this it seemed preferable to seek other ways of meeting the needs of the slow-learning pupils. It should also be noted that no instances were observed of separate classes without interaction with the main school and general teaching; it seemed that most schools, while appreciating the need for special classes for some pupils, also recognized the need for interaction with the rest of the school. There was a third form of organization: mixed-ability teaching without any special support for slow learners except what could be provided by the teacher *within* the class organization. A cynic might regard this as a non-organization for slow learners! Whatever the merits of mixed-ability teaching for pupils making normal progress in the normal curriculum (and they are many), it was the considered opinion of the project team that they had not observed the curricular needs of slow learners being satisfactorily met within this kind of school organization.

In special schools organization was almost universally based upon classes taught by a 'class' teacher over the range of basic subjects and general studies, including social studies. Teaching by 'specialist' teachers was limited to home economics, woodwork and metalwork, except for a few schools with visiting specialists for art, music or physical education. Within the schools, at secondary level, individual teachers sometimes concentrated on certain aspects of curriculum though it did not necessarily follow that they had special training in the chosen area. A similar kind of organization prevailed in separate departments for slow learners in primary and secondary schools, in the latter with more direct access to specially trained teachers.

Curriculum for slow learners

The curriculum for slow learners tended to reflect the principles of school organization. In schools with mixed-ability teaching it was difficult to detect any special curriculum for slow learners, who tended to follow the curriculum of their class or group, with modification (where this existed) mainly in the follow-up work to lesson presentation, and in the teacher's willingness to accept a lower standard of work from slow learners in the group. In other situations, attempts were made to relate the curriculum to the needs of the slow learners. In primary schools the best description of the curriculum would be concentration on basic subjects balanced by broad fields of study in one form or another. This accounted for 70 per cent of primary-school curricula. In special schools this description could be applied to 95 per cent of curricula. The curriculum for slow learners in secondary schools retained the concentration on basic subjects, but also outside these the traditional subject divisions were more often retained. Over 70 per cent of secondary-school curricula fitted this description. In all types of school there were examples of attempts to experiment with the curriculum but they were minority occurrences not typical of the prevailing curricular situation.

In all types of school it was claimed that continuous assessment was the basis of curriculum evaluation and that individual pupil records kept track of assessment. In practice records were almost entirely limited to end-of-term general reports and individual records of reading recognition tests. In all, 92 per cent of primary, 65 per cent of secondary and 62 per cent of special schools claimed to be making use of standardized tests of intelligence and attainments as part of the records. This claim was not substantiated by either the extent or quality of the records seen. The best of the records showed a good account of pupils' attainment, but contained little about the curriculum and teaching offered to the slow learners as they progressed through the schools.

Curriculum resources in the schools

In developing good curricula, schools must exploit features of their buildings and sites, of the local environment and the local community. The quality of the links between these and classroom learning is vital in work with slow learners and requires the use of modern audio-visual and reproductive equipment.

OUTSIDE FACILITIES ON SITE

Gardening or rural science facilities were available in 61 per cent of special and 53 per cent of secondary schools, but in only 10 per cent of primary schools. Accommodation for some livestock appeared in a third of all types of school. In the ordinary schools, good use was made of these facilities in work with slow learners. Outside covered areas were infrequently provided – they were found in only 10 per cent of secondary and special schools, and 5 per cent of primary schools. Provision of swimming pools was better – at 35 per cent for primary, 29 per cent for secondary and 28 per cent for special schools.

ACCOMMODATION

In 80 per cent of all schools, classroom accommodation was predominantly traditional. There were open-plan classrooms in only 5 per cent of primary schools, and 2 per cent of special schools, and there were none in secondary schools. Traditional classrooms with some open areas figured in 15 per cent of primary and special schools and 19 per cent of secondary schools. There was a widespread opinion among teachers that open-plan design was unsuitable for slow learners. If this view is correct, this factor may have contributed to the infrequent appearance of such classrooms in a sample of schools selected for successful work with slow-learning pupils. School halls were available in 97 per cent of schools, and in only 1 per cent of the sample was the hall shared. However, in half the primary

Table 1 Provision and use of specialist rooms or areas (rounded percentages of schools)

	PRIMARY		SECONDARY		SPECIAL
		Used by slow		Used by slow	
	Provided	learners	Provided	learners	Provided
Art	57	55	100	99	66
Commercial studies	1	1	66	43	2
Drama	1	1	25	25	2
Engineering	1	1	44	38	4
Home economics	8	8	86	86	81
Light craft	32	32	72	71	59
Metalwork	4	3	86	86	40
Music	17	17	85	81	2
Needlework	36	33	89	84	74
Pottery	43	39	91	86	77
Technical drawing	1	1	85	62	2
Woodwork	23	20	90	90	78
Activity area	24	23	11	11	35
Gymnasium	31	31	93	93	43
Language laboratory	2	2	34	15	4
Learning resources centre	15	14	15	15	2
Lecture theatre	1	1	27	25	2
Library	74	70	99	93	43
Model flat	2	1	53	51	46
Science laboratory	7	6	99	94	3

and special schools the use of halls for meals took them out of curricular use for about two hours each day, and the same happened in a third of the secondary schools. In 90 per cent of primary schools and 83 per cent of special schools, the hall was used as a gymnasium, as happened also in 22 per cent of secondary schools. This, of course, is a further restriction on the use of the hall for other curricular activities.

The availability of accommodation for specialist teaching is set out in Table 1. There is a critical interaction between the curriculum of a school and the facilities for specialist teaching which becomes more marked as pupils advance in secondary education. The disadvantage of primary schools may be less than it appears from the figures. Many of the specialist activities may be unsuited to the primary curriculum, or may be followed at a level which does not require specialist accommodation as an essential. This is not necessarily true of special schools which provide for substantial numbers of secondary-age pupils. Without making detailed comment, it can be construed from Table 1 that, apart from home economics, secondary pupils in special schools are less well provided for in many areas than slow learners in secondary schools. This lack of specialist accommodation is undoubtedly a factor in the low recruitment of specialist subject teachers in special schools, which deprives slow learners of contact with teachers who are not only experts but also enthusiasts for their specialism. Conversely, and as indicated by the usage column for secondary schools, contact with specialist teachers is one of the advantages of providing for slow learners within the ordinary school.

LOCAL FACILITIES

Variety in curriculum is limited by the facilities to which any school has access. Table 2 sets out the situation in the project schools.

Age, physical maturity and mental development of the pupil determine the suitability of some of the activities indicated in Table 2. This is reflected in the differences between primary and secondary schools, and is also a factor in the special schools where there are numbers of primary-age pupils. Similarly, access may often be determined by the distance which pupils may be expected to travel, and by the availability of transport under direct school control, a situation exceptionally rare in primary schools and attained in only 40 per cent of secondary schools and 51 per cent of special schools.

Secondary schools use the following facilities at least 10 per cent less with slow learners than with other pupils: mountains, field centres, inland water, fishing, youth hostels, commercial concerns, places of

Table 2 Local facilities useful in the curriculum: schools' access and use (rounded percentages of schools)

| | PRIMARY | | SECONDARY | | SPECIAL |
	Access	Used with slow learners	Access	Used with slow learners	Access
Countryside	91	88	94	91	97
Mountains	24	19	52	42	48
Coast	45	41	68	60	67
Nature reserve	44	41	50	46	59
Parks	75	69	77	68	88
Field centre	27	24	65	51	42
Outdoor pursuit centre	10	8	47	40	38
Camping facilities	25	20	63	54	66
Inland water	39	33	66	53	57
Fishing water	24	19	55	42	59
Other open spaces	70	64	80	76	83
Youth hostel	13	9	55	40	48
Industry	45	40	90	81	84
Commercial concerns	34	22	79	64	67
Places of geographical interest	48	45	89	79	76
Places of historical interest	76	73	94	91	85
Theatre	49	43	84	61	69
Cinema	50	37	84	70	82
Art gallery	40	33	70	56	71
Museum	81	72	92	88	85
Zoo	66	63	65	60	73
Shopping area	76	66	91	79	94
Ice skating	5	3	28	22	22
Roller skating	4	2	20	15	19
Horse riding	8	3	39	30	34
Swimming baths	75	67	86	76	86
Youth clubs	8	7	37	36	45
School transport	1	–	40	–	51

geographical interest, theatre, cinema, art gallery, shopping area and swimming baths. In primary schools use is more equitable, only commercial concerns, cinema and shopping area showing a 10 per cent deficit for slow learners. For all facilities except the countryside, use in special schools is higher by at least 10 per cent than use for slow learners in primary schools, though this may be influenced by the wider age-range of special-school pupils. Differences between secondary-school slow learners and special schools are less marked. Using the 10 per cent differential special schools make more use of nature reserves, parks, camping, fishing, cinema, art gallery, zoo, shopping area and swimming; they make less use of field centres, outdoor centres and places of historical or geographical interest, though the differential is lower and special schools appear to have less access than secondary schools to many of these facilities.

The situation shown in the table is clear: primary, secondary and special schools could all improve their use of local facilities in the curriculum for slow learners. Research literature* suggests that slow learners move about the environment less than their 'normal' peers and, in failing to exploit the environment fully, schools may be losing an opportunity for compensatory education. Though there is still room for improvement even in special schools, the curriculum in these schools appears to be more outward-looking than that in primary or secondary schools.

TEACHING EQUIPMENT

If an outward-looking curriculum is to contribute to classroom learning for slow learners, it is essential to have adequate links between out-of-school experience and class work, involving language, concept formation, imagery and imagination, as well as experience contributing to social perspective and awareness. Audio-visual and reproductive equipment and teaching machines help to make these essential links. Here, concern is with the availability and use of equipment in the project schools, and the situation is shown in Table 3.

First, Table 3 may be examined in terms of the overall possession of teaching equipment. A main point concerns the low provision of cine, instant-picture and still cameras. These, properly exploited, provide a vital link between out-of-school experience and classroom learning which the data suggest may not be fully exploited by the schools. Connected with this is the low provision of 8 mm cine and loop projectors in primary and special schools. A similar comment is valid on the low provision of portable, battery tape-recorders which are an audio-link with out-of-school activities. These comments are less pertinent to secondary schools,

* Summary in W. K. Brennan, *Shaping the Education of Slow Learners* (Routledge & Kegan Paul, 1974).

Table 3 Teaching equipment: possession and use by schools (rounded percentages of schools)

| | PRIMARY | | SECONDARY | | SPECIAL |
	Possession	Use with slow learners	Possession	Use with slow learners	Possession
Audio aids					
Radio	100	92	97	87	99
Tape recorder (non-portable)	90	85	99	97	96
Tape recorder (mains, portable)	81	72	86	76	78
Tape recorder (battery, portable)	52	47	68	61	45
Tape player	18	18	26	24	15
Record player (mono)	97	89	97	91	98
Record player (stereo)	24	23	46	37	21
Visual aids					
Filmstrip/slide projector	88	78	98	92	86
Cine projector (8 mm)	10	5	39	33	27
Loop projector	13	10	66	50	11
Overhead projector	23	16	88	68	26
Episcope	12	9	46	30	16
Audio-visual aids					
Cine projector (16 mm)	46	38	98	88	77
Television	93	90	99	96	89
Videotape recorder	1	1	33	26	19
Closed circuit TV: school	1	1	7	5	1
Closed circuit TV: local education authority centre	5	5	8	7	4
Reproductive equipment					
Still camera	16	12	64	46	48
Instant-picture camera	4	4	15	12	14
Cine camera	10	6	46	30	32
Typewriter (other than office)	17	13	79	61	53
Duplicator: spirit	79	66	95	69	83
Duplicator: ink	85	45	89	61	60
Photocopier	26	15	89	52	30
Printing press	1	1	35	17	13
Teaching machines					
Manual	13	12	32	29	42
Electronic	10	10	7	6	22

but apply directly to special schools and even more so to primary schools. It is with young children, and with older slow learners, all in the concrete phase of learning, that the positive link with outside activities may be most important, and better provision of the vital linking equipment may be critical in any attempt to improve teaching and the curriculum.

Another comment relates to tape players. The low provision of players compared with tape recorders suggests that the schools have not exploited the economy of the player's potential for good reproduction at lower cost, or have thought in 'sets' of recorder plus player as an economical way of using resources.

Photocopiers, too, are now reasonably accessible and cheap, and are a welcome addition for use in concrete modes of learning. Primary and special schools have not yet fully appreciated this point in practice. Video recorders are expensive and just beginning to appear in these schools. They can add considerable flexibility to timetabling and, properly exploited, can make main-channel educational programmes viable for pupil-viewers other than the intended audience (bearing in mind the terms of educational broadcasting recording concessions and retention rights). The emergence of a reliable cassette videotape recorder will simplify the use of this equipment which has much to offer in schools and with slow learners.

Secondly, Table 3 may be examined in terms of the comparative provision of equipment. In this summary of the situation, differences in the percentages of possession between different types of school have been ignored where the difference is less than 10 per cent. Using this criterion the following facts emerge:

1 Primary-school provision *less* than secondary-school: battery, portable tape recorder; stereo record player; filmstrip/slide projector; 8 mm and 16 mm cine projectors; loop and overhead projectors; episcope; videotape recorder; still, instant-picture and cine cameras; typewriter; spirit duplicator; photocopier; printing press; manual teaching machine
2 Primary-school provision *more* than secondary-school: none
3 Primary-school provision *less* than special-school: 8 mm and 16 mm projectors; videotape recorder; still, instant-picture and cine cameras; typewriter; printing press; manual and electronic teaching machines
4 Primary-school provision *more* than special-school: ink duplicator
5 Special-school provision *less* than secondary-school: battery, portable tape recorder; tape player; stereo record player; filmstrip/slide, loop and overhead projectors; 8 mm and 16 mm cine projectors;

episcope; television; videotape recorder; still and cine cameras; typewriter; spirit and ink duplicators; photocopier; printing press
6 Special-school provision *more* than secondary-school: manual and electronic teaching machines.

Capitation resources are more restricted in primary and special schools than in secondary schools, and a case could be made for some reappraisal of this situation. Nevertheless, within the overall figures, some primary and special schools had succeeded in building up a collection of equipment which would bear comparison with any secondary school; clearly, even in current circumstances, the problem of assembling adequate teaching equipment in primary and special schools can be resolved. Nor should it be overlooked that the priorities are *not* the same in the three types of school and that essential curricular or method differences will be reflected in the pattern of demand for equipment. An outstanding example of this is the marked superiority of secondary schools in the provision of typewriters. This is almost totally accounted for by the inclusion of typewriting courses in secondary schools, and would be inappropriate in primary or special schools.

Thirdly, Table 3 may be examined in terms of the use of facilities with slow learners in primary and secondary schools, compared with special schools, where it seems reasonable to assume that facilities are available to all the pupils, as all are slow learners. Differences in possession of facilities and usage with slow learners have been ignored if less than 10 per cent. The following facts emerge:

1 Primary-school facilities used *less* with slow learners: filmstrip/slide projector; spirit and ink duplicators; photocopier
2 Primary-school use with slow learners *less* than special-school: tape recorder; 8 mm and 16 mm projectors; overhead projector; videotape recorder; still, instant-picture and cine cameras; typewriter; spirit and ink duplicators; photocopier; printing press; manual and electronic teaching machines
3 Primary-school use with slow learners *more* than special-school: none
4 Primary-school use with slow learners *less* than secondary-school: mains and battery, portable tape recorders; stereo record player; film/slide projector; 8 mm and 16 mm cine projectors; loop and overhead projectors; episcope; videotape recorder; still and cine cameras; typewriter; ink duplicator; photocopier; printing press; manual teaching machine
5 Primary-school use with slow learners *more* than secondary-school: none

6 Secondary-school facilities used *less* with slow learners: radio; mains, portable tape recorder; loop and overhead projectors; episcope; 16 mm cine projector; still and cine cameras; typewriter; spirit and ink duplicators; photocopier; printing press

7 Secondary-school use with slow learners *less* than special-school: radio; spirit duplicator; manual and electronic teaching machines

8 Secondary-school use with slow learners *more* than special-school: battery, portable tape recorder; stereo record player; loop and overhead projectors; episcope; 16 mm cine projector; photocopier.

Though curriculum differences, together with differences in the age or maturity of pupils, undoubtedly affect the patterns of use of equipment in the schools, some points require comment. The greater heterogeneity of slow learners compared with their normal peers; the need to produce special teaching materials which will extend the content and objectives of ordinary curricula to slow learners; the need to produce learning materials at low reading ages; the need to use more graphic approaches in communicating with slow-learning pupils; the need to produce learning materials with finer grading than that required for normal pupils; as well as the need to provide the slow learner with a more direct and specific relationship between school tasks and his personal experience – all these suggest that tape recorders, cameras, projectors, duplicators and other aids, have a more substantial contribution to make to teaching the slow learner than they have to teaching his normal peers. This is certainly not reflected in the data from Table 3 which suggest that more thought and effort is required if audio-visual and reproductive equipment are to make their maximum contribution to curriculum content and teaching methods in the education of slow-learning pupils. Part of the differential between primary and the other schools reflects the less liberal provision of equipment as well as the scarcity of suitable 'software' for young children. However, there is a place for experiment with reproductive equipment, particularly in the visual–perceptual and language area of the curriculum. Similar comment could be made about the curriculum for younger pupils in special schools, though the table indicates rather better usage of equipment here compared with primary schools. Compared with secondary schools, the superiority of special-school usage is less marked. Secondary schools make more use of portable tape recorders and projectors; special schools, more use of radio, spirit duplicators and teaching machines, to some extent with their younger pupils in curricular areas not appropriate for secondary schools. The fact that most special schools span the full primary and secondary age-range makes it difficult to achieve direct comparison of use with the other types of school.

Yet there can be no evading the overall impression of less extensive use of equipment in the teaching of slow learners. Curriculum content, doubtful suitability of materials and inequities of capitation may have something to do with this. But the motivational needs of slow learners, their need for repetition and reinforcement of learning, as well as the value of linking school learning with out-of-school experience, suggest that more extensive and creative use of teaching aids would be one means of resolving their learning problems.

A qualification should be made in considering the points made in this chapter. It is clear from the earlier description (pages 12–13) that the project schools were neither a random nor a representative sample of schools working with slow learners. They are simply a selection of schools considered successful with slow learners and, within the limits set by the method of selection, they represent examples of good contemporary practice. No other claim is made for them.

III. A selective review of curriculum literature

Introduction

This chapter has two main objectives. First, it discusses literature on the curriculum in a way which may indicate how thinking in the project has been influenced by the literature. Secondly, it attempts to discuss the literature in a way which will demonstrate its relevance to the work of teachers of slow learners and to the education of their pupils. Selection has been influenced by experience in the project schools which strongly suggests that:

1   Most teachers of slow learners would benefit from wider acquaintance with the general literature on curriculum development
2   The development of comprehensive secondary schools raises new and urgent questions about the need for a common-core curriculum
3   There is a need for more emphasis on curriculum objectives expressed as observable and verifiable aspects of the knowledge, skills, attitudes and values which the pupil is expected to derive from the teaching and learning situations to which he is exposed in the school.

Specific literature on the slow learner

Consideration of the education of slow learners began with early concern about the education of mentally handicapped children, and this concern originated in the nineteenth century with medical men such as Itard and Seguin,[1] rather than with educationists. If this seems remote, then Ball[2] has shown how the older ideas relate to more recent development in the curriculum for slow learners, and the early developments are well summarized by Kirk and Johnson.[3] Brennan[4] has summarized in detail the specific literature on the curriculum for slow learners, and that literature is outlined here in general terms.

Approaches to the curriculum for slow learners may be classified under seven headings:

1 *Sensory training.* In this group are works which emphasize sensory training using concrete activities to promote dexterity and lead to use of basic subjects (Montessori; Descoeudres; Itard; Seguin).[5]

2 *Watered-down curriculum.* This group includes approaches to the curriculum for slow learners which emphasize traditional 'academic' subjects, reduced in content and academic level to match the assumed limitation of slow learners (Inskeep; Baron; Hill; Cheshire Education Committee).[6]

3 *Concrete use of basic subjects.* This approach emphasizes practical activities in basic subjects, closely correlated and related to thinking and problem-solving by pupils (Duncan).[7]

4 *Core programmes.* Core programmes usually emphasize social competence and occupational efficiency, and concentrate on 'life functions' (Hungerford, Depruso and Rossenzweig; Goldstein and Segal).[8]

5 *Units of experience.* The units are designed to secure interest and motivate the pupil through concern with contemporary problems closely related to the developmental level of the pupil (Martens; Featherstone; Ingram).[9]

6 *Broad subject fields.* This group emphasizes broadly defined subject fields, such as communication, literacy, numeracy, social competence, creative arts, etc., stressing the interaction between learning and use of knowledge and skills (Kirk and Johnson; Tansley and Gulliford; Segal; Department of Education and Science; Schools Council; Bell; Williams).[10]

7 *Education of special groups.* These works are concerned with the development of restricted, special programmes related to specific factors believed to be the cause of learning difficulties – for example brain injury, visual–motor deficiency, perceptual difficulties (Strauss and Lehtinen; Tansley; Benyon; Chaney and Kephart; Frostig and Maslow; Brennan, Jackson and Reeve; McCreesh and Maher).[11]

In addition, a number of texts from American literature contain useful summaries of approaches to the curriculum for slow learners. Kirk and Johnson[12] present brief but useful historical summaries, review modern approaches to teaching the slow learner and discuss educational programmes in the context of the pupil's development. Wallin[13] includes a thorough discussion of varied aspects of curriculum backed up by an extensive bibliography. Stevens[14] develops a pertinent summary of curriculum literature noting the 'high-flown' language and 'over broad' nature of some statements as well as the overlap in ideas and the ambiguity which arises from differences in terminology. Johnson[15] reviews broad curriculum objectives for slow learners and considers curriculum at primary-, secondary- and high-school levels as well as in subject areas.

In Britain some attempts have been made to discuss the curriculum for slow learners. The Department of Education and Science in *Slow Learners at School*[16] attempts to outline the approach to the curriculum in developmental terms, and stresses personal skills and values in the curriculum, but is somewhat restrictive in discussing the role of science and humanities in the curriculum for slow learners. Gulliford[17] sets out developmental aspects of curriculum in more detail, with attempts to define the behavioural objectives to be attained at each level from infant to secondary stage. Brennan,[18] summarizing literature, notes a movement away from a subject-orientated curriculum towards a concern for the slow learner in his own right, as a person involved in relationships with others. Brennan also notes the lack of concern with behavioural outcomes or objectives in the literature on curriculum for slow learners and regrets the absence of detailed analysis of curriculum along lines indicated in modern approaches to curriculum development. He notes the exception of Taylor,[19] who identifies curriculum levels in compensatory education as:

1 Definition of general aims
2 Definition of general objectives
3 Translation of general into specific objectives
4 Identification of learning experiences required for achievement of specific objectives
5 Translation of learning experiences into organized topics or themes to be presented in the classroom.

Gulliford[20] outlines the application of steps 1 to 4 to the education of slow learners. More recently, McCreesh and Maher[21] have attempted to relate the Taylor model to specific teaching with the objective of assisting pupils to overcome perceptual difficulties. Brennan,[22] in a wider discussion, has extended the model, stressed the need to break down terminal objectives into intermediate objectives which match developmental levels in pupils, and has indicated the central importance of recording and feedback of information in this type of curriculum development.

General literature: the curriculum

A number of contributions in the general field of curriculum development are relevant to the curriculum for slow learners, particularly as they identify a central problem. If the curriculum is to be differentiated in order to meet the special needs of slow learners, than at what point (if any) does that very differentiation become a separatist device, in that it 'cuts off' the slow learner from the common aspects of curriculum which contribute to cultural and social cohesion in our society? Put another way, if the transmission of some degree of common culture through a common curriculum is one purpose of education, at what point does the differentiated curriculum for the slow learner depart from that purpose? If so, should it? By what right is any child denied access to any area of human knowledge? The specific literature on the slow learner shows little awareness of these important questions.

The view that differentiated curriculum is divisive and constitutes a special problem in a society claiming to be democratic is widely held and well stated by Gardner.[23] He sees education systems serving as a 'sorting-out' process, first deciding 'who shall go to college' and, through this, determining 'who shall manage society'. Though Gardner wrote about the North American system, his views reflect thinking in the United Kingdom which has supported the development of comprehensive schools. The 'sorting' is there in both systems, not necessarily as a conscious objective of the educational process, but certainly as a fact of the function of the systems. White[24] goes further than Gardner. He takes a radical standpoint which he defines as a belief that the aim of education is to produce a society in which everyone is acquainted with the higher culture. At present this is not so. There *are* two forms of education: the academic leading to higher education; and the rest. For White the Schools Council has become an agent of this separation, a contention he supports by analysis of the Council's output. But what of all the teacher activity fostered by the Council? This is all about *means*, says White, with little thought devoted to the *ends* of education; and it is ends which matter to the radical. The lack of thought about ends and purpose allows the curricular separation (Gardner's 'sorting') to persist unchallenged. White's solution is a compulsory, common curriculum, through which all will gain appropriate, not necessarily identical, acquaintance with the higher culture.

Taylor[25] examined the curriculum for the average child in the secondary-modern school. First, he identified the 'practical' approach to the curriculum. Given emphasis by the recognition in the Hadow

Report of 1926[26] that the academic 'grammar-school' curriculum was unsuitable for the majority of pupils, the 'practical' or 'technical' curriculum of secondary-modern schools was traced back to the curricula developed in 'higher-grade schools' after 1902 as the academic curricula became the prerogative of the new 'secondary schools'. Secondly, Taylor identified the contribution of 'progressive' educationists from Montessori, through Dewey to Neill. The effect of their ideas made 'practical' education 'child centred', stressed that curricula should meet personal needs, and introduced an aesthetic and creative content related to spontaneous activities. But thirdly, Taylor identified the growth of a reactive 'tough-minded' approach to secondary-modern curricula, represented by a concern for standards in basic literacy and by the entry of the more competent pupils for public examinations.

Bantock[27] took up the question of a satisfactory curriculum for the majority of pupils, whom he contended were ill-served by the 'watered-down academic education we still provide as the core of the curriculum'. Bantock uses historical, literary, psychological, linguistic and cultural evidence to support his view of a majority of the school population operating at the level of Piaget's concrete operations and Bernstein's restricted language codes throughout the years of secondary education. His proposed curriculum extends the concept of 'practicality' by rejecting the idea that it implies 'undertakings of limited vision and imaginative poverty', and includes popular entertainment, life skills, and consideration of human relationships and marriage. Allied to these is the concept of an artistic–aesthetic element in the curriculum, taking in the modern cultural forms of television, film and the popular press, while extending work in movement, music, art and crafts. Though not rejecting the training in reading which he sees as a 'fundamental discipline' of traditional education, Bantock proposes the 'art of movement with its emphasis on motor skills, communal participation and opportunity to develop perception and empathy' as the 'fundamental discipline' of revised curriculum. English is to be approached in a similar way (following Holbrook[28]) and as part of a training in communication embracing all modern mass forms and inculcating a critical attitude to their output and use.

The closely argued case presented by Bantock is consistent with the thinking of many successful teachers of slow learners. They will welcome his clearly stated assertions about his curriculum:

1 That more able children will achieve more in the curriculum
2 That the specific, concrete nature of crafts and associated arts is

especially valuable for children more efficient in concrete and practical
areas

3 That it is not an 'inferior sop for the inadequate' but 'provides an
entry into many of the greatest riches of our civilization'

4 That such a curriculum can operate and be effective at many different
levels.

Equally honest is Bantock's statement of the two basic premises of his
approach:

1 That heredity ineluctably determines differences in intellectual and
affective capacity among children

2 That many children in schools are 'grossly and palpably under-
functioning'.

Given the division between academic education and the kind of general
education which he proposes, Bantock apparently accepts it as an axiom,
as his argument places little stress on the need for any common element
to unite the 'two curricula'. To some extent Bantock's position may be
regarded as a reaction against views such as those proposed by Hirst,[29]
and Hirst and Peters,[30] and specifically opposed to Hirst's assertion that
'we must get away completely from the idea that linguistic and abstract
forms of thought are not for some people'.[31]

In general, Hirst's view is that education should have as its central
objective the development of 'a rational mind'. This does not mean that
affective, moral, social and physical development are ignored, but that
these are pursued in a way related to the pupil's progress in rational
understanding, to which, ideally, they should contribute. Hirst puts his
view explicitly:

> If once the central objectives of rationality are submerged, or are
> given up so that these other pursuits take over, then I suggest that
> the school has betrayed its educational trust, no matter how suc-
> cessful it may be in these other respects, and no matter how laudable
> these other ends may be in themselves.[32]

The other pursuits or ends are a variety of interesting and worth-while
activities, vocational skills and many forms of socialization: all objectives
which figure highly in discussion of the education of slow learners! The
implication of this view is stated with equal emphasis:

> If the acquisition of certain fundamental elements of knowledge is
> necessary to the achievement of the rational mind in some particular
> respect, then these at any rate cannot but be universal objectives for

the curriculum. If the objectives of our education differ for sections of our society so as to ignore any of these elements for some of our pupils, either because they are considered too difficult, or for some reason they are thought less important for these pupils, then we are denying to them certain basic ways of rational development and we have indeed got inequality of educational opportunity of the most far-reaching kind.[33]

There is much here to trouble most teachers of slow learners. What if, in resolving the pupil's learning difficulties, curriculum omissions make it more difficult for him to establish worth-while contact with his normal peers, or with his natural and social environment? Hirst at least makes a start to answering this question. The purpose of the curriculum is not the production of specialists in different forms of knowledge; subjects can be studied in different ways, with different emphasis. Nor is the object to amass details of knowledge or technique, or knowledge with everyday usefulness. The objective is that the pupils should begin to think in a distinctive way; acquire a hold on features which distinctively characterize different forms of knowledge; and develop autonomous functioning using relevant concepts and criteria.

In stressing the subject approach (which he clearly advocates) Hirst notes the tendency to identify subject teaching with formal teaching, suggesting that this is not inevitable and certainly not desirable. He also gives special meaning to 'subject' by categorizing knowledge as: mathematics, physical science, human science and history, literature and fine arts, morals, religion and philosophy. Advocating new teaching approaches, Hirst recognizes the need for new courses which involve his central, logical elements, that 'all pupils can take successfully', though he admits to our inexperience in designing such courses. He points out that the courses need not be identical for all pupils, even given common objectives and a high degree of common content. He says there are 'no adequate grounds for saying this is impossible when we have in fact spent so little of our effort trying to achieve this'. Commenting on the topic approach to this problem, Hirst is critical. He sees the topic approach as less systematic in developing understanding, less flexible in permitting choice of content aimed directly at central, logical concepts, and more difficult to handle efficiently in the classroom. For Hirst, the central justification made for the topic approach is not the contribution it makes to rationality, but in that the suitable choice of topics 'can overcome many motivational problems with less able pupils and much practical and useful information and many useful skills can be acquired easily and efficiently when approached in this way'. This justification Hirst finds less than acceptable.

Some interesting similarities exist between the apparently opposed views of Bantock and Hirst. Both accept that there are marked differences between individual pupils which affect learning – one holding this view explicitly, the other more implicitly. Both agree that the problems are more to do with what should be taught and how, rather than with the organization of education, though neither appears to admit that those who stress organization are often concerned with the same objectives as themselves. There are also basic differences which highlight the weaknesses of the positions. Bantock focuses on differences of unchangeable heredity; Hirst ignores the possibility of their existence. Hirst stresses the need to seek common, cohesive features of curriculum which will contribute to cultural assimilation and social unity. Bantock does not recognize the need for such a curriculum objective. Bantock proposes an approach to intellect through aesthetic–artistic activities. Hirst makes contribution to intellect the criterion by which to test such activities for inclusion in the curriculum. Bantock is explicit in identifying the historical, literary, cultural, psychological and sociological sources of support for his argument. Hirst is more implicit and general and, to that extent, as stated, his case may appear the weaker.

Shipman[34] points out an unexpected aspect of differentiated curricula in relation to the reorganization of secondary education on comprehensive principles. He notes two important movements pressing on the curriculum: progressive pressures for 'relevant' education for less academic pupils, crystallized in the Newsom Report,[35] and traditional academic standards crystallized in the external examination system. Two institutions are involved, the universities and the Schools Council. Shipman notes how both institutions are concerned with both sources of pressure. The universities are active in promoting experiment in new approaches to curriculum for non-examination pupils, though they are at the same time traditional and conservative in their requirements for those pupils who will become university students. Similarly, the working papers from the Schools Council, relevant, experimental and outgoing, contrast with what Shipman sees as the traditionalist approach of the examination-oriented documents from the same source. Though concerned mainly with secondary schools, Shipman suggests that a similar situation exists in primary schools, where the prevalence of streaming ensures that differences exist in the curricula of higher- and lower-stream children; these differences, though possibly reduced by the decline of selection for secondary schools, nevertheless still persist. Within the comprehensive school, the thesis goes, the 'academic' or 'grammar' stream, oriented to largely unchanged external examinations syllabuses, continues its traditional subject-oriented curriculum by means of formal teaching methods. In contrast with this, under the influence of the Newsom Report (which accepted differentiated curricula), the non-examination streams, groups or sets pursue active, outgoing, experimental curricula stressing personal or social objectives, often at the expense of intellectual content or standards, though highly charged with relevance to life, interest and motivation. Leaving aside the merits or demerits of the two approaches, Shipman makes his important point that, within the comprehensive school, this curriculum dichotomy may separate the two groups of pupils both more clearly and more effectively than the separate secondary schools did: hence Shipman's title 'Curriculum for inequality?'.

There is an interesting but urgent irony in the idea that the comprehensive schools should, because of curriculum developments which have powerful arguments based upon relevance to support them, become an effective means of continuing a social, cultural and educational dichotomy which they were created, at least in part, to resolve. Further, as slow learners are on one side of the division, the consequences of the situation are urgent and relevant for their teachers.

Shipman points out that his thesis is not an attack on either side of the divide. He welcomes the changes following from Newsom and the emergence of new, relevant and exciting curricula for the average and below average pupil; but he stresses that relevance and interest should not exclude academic disciplines, while academic courses themselves could be improved by assimilating some of the new methods from 'the other side'. Lawton[36] also supports Shipman's view of the danger of lack of intellectual content in the new, outward-looking courses following from the Newsom Report. He is specific: unless the objective of democratic citizenship is part of an educational programme involving at least some initiation into the social sciences, then 'a civic approach to secondary education becomes no more than indoctrination or manipulation'. Strong words – but words to be taken seriously by teachers of slow learners.

Neither Shipman nor Lawton says much about how the dichotomy is to be resolved, though Lawton has recently made some interesting proposals which are discussed below. But the first step in resolving a problem is to define it clearly. This they have done – especially Shipman. The magnitude of the problem posed is seen in the fact that at the time of writing, several years later, resolution seemed no nearer. Nor, for that matter, were we much nearer the kind of courses required by Bantock and Hirst. Indeed, to leap ahead in this narrative, most teachers of slow learners in the project schools appeared totally committed to curricula focused on the personal needs of their pupils and were almost unaware of the potential (and often actual) curriculum dichotomy existing in their own schools.

It is interesting to note that Schools Council Working Paper No. 2, *Raising the School Leaving Age*,[37] made pertinent suggestions which might have contributed to lessening this curriculum dichotomy, fostered the approach suggested by Hirst and made unnecessary some of the criticisms of the new courses made by Lawton. This working paper rejected the view that slow learners are not interested in ideas, that they cannot verbalize or handle abstractions, that they make choices through immediate satisfactions and are only interested in people or concrete situations. The rejection of this view of the slow learner was based on evidence from further and adult education and from the experience of secondary schools where slow learners stayed on for extended education. Also quoted was the experience from primary schools that

> practically all pupils can acquire insight into abstract ideas and a capacity to work with them (particularly by oral means) if doors are opened through the use of teaching methods which build on the pupils' present experience and supply new forms of experience which help them to discover for themselves the power of their own minds.

The curriculum suggested was to achieve organic unity through the study of man and his needs as reflected in human society, with English, history, geography and religious studies combined in new humanities courses, bringing in the social sciences. These were not to be mere 'life-adjustment' courses but studies of practical situations leading to generalizations and the formation of concepts. Unfortunately, follow-up to Working Paper No. 2 was not good; the views have not been given practical development (in the working paper they were regarded as almost too revolutionary to be easily or quickly adopted) and the main problems remain unresolved.

Some implications

Consideration of Working Paper No. 2 and possible implications arising from it suggest that the curriculum dichotomy might be resolved by attention to *teaching method* – broadly interpreted as the total strategies of teaching and learning employed by the teacher (or teachers) to ensure that pupils achieve balanced cognitive, affective, motor, social and practical objectives. Such an approach would be consistent with Hirst's view of the need to achieve objectives of logical thought; and it could also encompass Bantock's ideas, as a most appropriate way of providing concrete experience leading to generalizations, concepts and thinking processes for pupils who have difficulty in these areas of behaviour. Viewed in this way, with emphasis on method, the ideas of both Hirst and Bantock have something in common with the curricula advocated by Duncan,[38] who used the idea of 'concrete intelligence' formulated by Alexander[39] to generate activities based on practical situations closely related to art and craft in order to develop thinking and problem-solving for his educationally subnormal pupils. The limited nature of Duncan's curriculum has been criticized and it has been suggested that his pupils were not typical slow learners (Kirk and Johnson; Tansley and Gulliford; Brennan).[40] Nevertheless he does offer one useful approach which may have value for some slow learners. Similarly, Bantock's stress on the value of movement is spelled out in much more detail, if less aesthetic–artistic, in the work of Kephart[41] and Chaney and Kephart.[42] Kephart sees movement, applied to the establishment of accurate and permanent body-image, as the essential requirement for the development of motor control, and the basis of perceptions of the world leading to rich and accurate concept formation. Frostig, in her work dealing with visual perception, develops the theme also, particularly in her discussion of the physical activity programmes which must accompany her perceptual programme (Frostig and Horne).[43] Tansley[44] and Brennan, Jackson and Reeve[45] have advocated similar approaches for motor-perceptual, and conceptual development.

Bantock, in his argument, indicates Piaget's developmental phases as one source for his idea of the concrete–aesthetic curriculum. Certainly this has validity, and more so when combined with Piaget's notion of thought as internalized action, which can be the unifying concept bringing together the approaches of Hirst, Bantock, Duncan, Kephart and Frostig. Most slow learners, initially, are at the level of Piaget's concrete operations, and learning situations *must* be presented in that mode, which for the teacher is a problem in method. Rich, concrete experience provides for a wide variety of perceptual learning based upon interaction between the pupil and his environment.

These inputs (or 'learnings') are represented mentally by the structures, or 'schemata' to use Piaget's term, which are constantly revised, re-arranged, extended or enriched through the process of assimilation–accommodation which is central to Piaget's view of learning. As individuals mature intellectually and become capable of function at Piaget's operational level of abstract thought, the structures established and refined at the concrete level provide the material operated upon by the maturing, logical mind of the adolescent. Even for the intellectually precocious primary-school pupil, little service is done by pressing premature development towards the formal level of operations, but most service by encouraging the widest, richest possible experience at the concrete level so that, with intellectual maturity, there is massive richness of structures or schemata for manipulation at the level of formal operations. Similar methodological considerations have relevance for older slow learners; for, even if it is admitted that some may never reach the level of formal operations, they gain from the richness established at the concrete level. Further support for this view appears in the work of Bruner,[46] as the positive attitudes to learning which are implied in the above approach could contribute to the emergence of 'intuitive' thinking at a later, more mature level, a possibility strongly implied in Bruner's work.

The above methodological approach offers a means of reconciling Bantock's stress on the concrete approach with Hirst's requirement that the development of a logical mind should be a central objective in the process of education. It will not, of itself, resolve the problem of the differentiation of curricula noted by Shipman nor satisfy the need for a common unifying element in the curricula for which Hirst seems to be searching. Something additional is required if this problem is to be resolved. That 'something' might well have been suggested in the work of Tansley and Gulliford,[47] elaborated and developed by Brennan.[48]

Tansley and Gulliford face up to the project versus subject dilemma, which is close to the dichotomy identified by Shipman. They point the dilemma as follows:

> If the curriculum content is compartmentalised into subjects it is less easy to provide those broad experiences and real-life situations which are so necessary. The importance of social education may be overlooked. If correlation is emphasised, the basic subjects are likely to suffer because of difficulty of control and continuity; teaching may become subservient to the project and not related to the individual.

These authors propose to resolve the dilemma for slow learners by a curriculum consisting of a central core of learning objectives which must be learned and understood permanently, surrounded by a periphery of objectives to be established at the level of 'awareness'. The parts are not to be independent for 'as the core develops, so the periphery widens, and as the child achieves command of the essential tools of learning he realises their usefulness. The interplay between core and periphery becomes more sensitive and apparent.' Brennan extends these ideas in two ways. First, he retains the idea of the 'understanding–awareness' dimension in objectives of knowledge but extends it to include skill objectives by proposing a 'mastery–familiarity' dimension. Secondly, he points out that, in the education of slow learners, there is no implied hierarchy in the understanding–awareness dimension or in the mastery–familiarity dimension. Nor is there any implied hierarchy between the two dimensions. Which dimension is more important, and which level within the dimension is to have precedence in formulating the objectives of learning should be determined by studying the needs of the pupil, not by any theoretical concept in the mind of the teacher. Brennan anticipates the operation of traditional teacher attitudes which would tend to give precedence to objectives involving 'understanding' or 'mastery'. He points out that, in certain circumstances, learning with objectives of 'awareness' or 'familiarity' may be the most important for the pupils. Slow learners need to be aware of many things they may not fully understand but which have central importance in ensuring that pupils are able to relate efficiently to their natural and social environments.

It should be noted at once that the understanding–awareness and mastery–familiarity balance does not introduce a new *principle* into the curriculum for slow learners. The principle applies to all curricula which are part of limited, formal, statutory education. Because such education is for a limited number of years, it is quite impossible for any school to teach, or for any pupil to learn, all that it would be beneficial to teach or learn. There is, therefore, inevitable selection – which is precisely why a curriculum needs to be thought out and developed. And for all pupils selection is not only a question of inclusion or exclusion of *areas* of knowledge or experience; there is the associated question of different *levels* of learning to be established in association with certain knowledge or experience objectives – which, again, is precisely what the understanding–awareness, etc., balance is about. Nor is the principle confined to the curriculum; it is a marked feature of life in a modern, complex, industrial–scientific society. No one (not even philosophers) can understand *every* aspect of the natural or social environment. In all kinds of ways – from the times of trains, through the working of the sewerage system, to the explanation of conditions in a space vehicle – people accept and rely upon explanations provided for them. The difference between a philosopher and a slow learner is not that one needs awareness and the other does not, but the fact that, because of different propensities for learning, allied to different interests and (possibly) education, the slow learner's understanding–awareness index *might* be rather more biased in the direction of awareness than the philosopher's! Practical teachers are unlikely to overlook this principle though it may be missed by theorists. And curricular theory needs to keep close to practice, for separation here has been identified by Schwab[49] as one reason for the moribund state of much of the discussion of the curriculum.

By making use of the concept of awareness the teacher may plan for the slow learner's achievement of curriculum objectives which allow him to relate and adjust to aspects of his environment which he does not (or even cannot) fully understand. In doing this slow learners often acquire insights which contribute to the emergence of 'intuitive' thinking as they mature, in the manner noted above (page 40). These insights extend the slow learner's awareness of his membership of society and they extend the possibility of areas of curriculum common to all pupils. Carefully handled, with appropriate selection of objectives and methods, the common curricular experiences should contribute to improved communication between slow learners and their normal peers as well as to improved mutual understanding and acceptance of each other's value. Such curricular developments could go far to reduce the dangerous curricular separation identified by Shipman.

The need for curriculum objectives

The criticism of Stevens[50] noted above, concerns the over-generalized discussion of the curriculum for slow learners which is a feature of the literature in the USA. Until recently, that criticism could have been made of similar literature in Britain. Cleugh, Segal, Bell and Williams[51] all provide excellent discussions of curricular aims, content and organization, but they have little to say about specific objectives to be achieved by the pupil as a result of the teaching to which he is to be exposed. According to Hirst[52] this is also a weakness of most general curricula in schools, and there is nothing in the experience of the project which contradicts this view. Hirst also points out that traditional subject approaches to curricula have a content which at least implies agreed objectives, but he argues that where content is set out in terms of projects and activities 'even this degree of specification may well be lacking'. A similar point is made by Tansley and Gulliford in their discussion of project versus subject organization quoted above.

One thing that has emerged from this review of literature is the importance of two associated developments if the education of slow learners is to be appropriate, effective in meeting their personal, social and intellectual needs, and at the same time to have points of contact with the education of average and above average pupils. First, success will not depend upon complexities of unassociated knowledge. It will depend more upon skill learning: skill learning, that is, not as an end in itself, but as a pertinent and appropriate approach to concept formation, sequential thinking and problem-solving behaviour. Through such an approach, skills are elaborated, integrated and generalized, following Kephart[53] who applies the learning principles of Hebb[54] and Harlow.[55] Secondly, if this is to become a reality, there must be great improvement in the precision with which the behavioural objectives of the curriculum are defined, both in terms of the *content* of behaviours and the *levels* at which they are to be established by the pupil.

Skills must be established before they can be elaborated, integrated and generalized, and this process is necessary if the learner is to acquire the conceptual insights which are part of generalization and the link between perceptual–motor activities and the cognitive process. Increased precision in defining behavioural outcomes of learning (curriculum objectives) is a prerequisite in seeking this kind of improvement in the curriculum for slow-learning pupils. Is there anything in the literature which could assist teachers in this?

There is, in fact, an extensive literature on the behavioural or objectives approach to the curriculum. *The Taxonomy of Educational Objectives* (Bloom; Krathwohl et al.)[56] sets out an extensive list of objectives, with examples, but may be too academic and too far removed from the activities of the classroom to have much effect on teacher behaviour. Much nearer to the classroom is the model proposed by Wheeler[57] which has been influenced by the work of Tyler[58] and Taba.[59] Wheeler's model has some advantages for the curriculum for slow learners in that it appears to be particularly suitable for skill learning and is consistent with the psychological principles of learning which should be applied in the teaching of children with learning difficulties.

Summarized, Wheeler's model involves the following stages in curriculum development:

1 *Statements of educational aims* which encompass philosophical/ethical values in education, and even beliefs, giving purpose to the process as well as shaping it.

2 *Translation of aims into statements of objectives* as observable, measurable or assessable, anticipated outcomes of the teaching–learning

process. And, further, the breakdown of 'terminal' objectives into 'mediate' objectives, consistent with the logical divisions of learning and assigned to appropriate stages in the pupil's personal development.

3   *The selection of learning experiences*, relevant to the objectives, which are consistent with principles of learning, and have validity, comprehensiveness, variety, suitability, pattern, relevance to life and potential for pupil participation in planning.

4   *Selection of content* consistent with the basic intellectual framework, capable of organization into appropriate themes or topics and offering alternative organizations or alternative items of content necessary if there is to be effective learning in the classroom.

5   *Organization of interaction of experience and content.* This implies basic decisions about, for example, subject, activity or core curricula; the interaction of these at different points; and identification and development of points of integration within the organization. Selection will be influenced both by the aims and objectives of the curriculum.

6   *Evaluation.* This process implies a continuous comparison of the anticipated or expected outcomes of the teaching–learning process with the actual outcomes observed in the behaviour of the pupils. It cannot exist in the absence of clearly defined behavioural objectives from stage 2 above. It also implies the existence of measurement or assessment as appropriate and the consideration of identified outcomes against the total experience and situation of the pupil. This, specifically, *is* the evaluation and ideally it should have an element of self-evaluation by the pupil.

7   *Feedback.* Feedback in the curriculum exists in two main senses. First, evaluation is used to monitor and refine the amount and quality of teaching, and to alter or refine objectives to make them more appropriate for the pupil. Secondly, in curriculum development, there is continuous interaction between the stages identified above, which are not logically or psychologically independent and continually influence each other.

An important aspect of Wheeler's work is his suggestion that stages 1, 2 and 3 of the curriculum are the concern of the school, regarded as an institution, while stages 4 and 5 can be determined only by the teacher in the classroom. At stages 6 and 7 the institution is once more involved and the process may in fact gain from an objectivity denied to the class teacher. Relevant also to this aspect of curriculum planning are questions about how far wider community involvement is desirable or possible in stages 1 to 3 and 6 and 7.

As noted above, the attraction of the objectives model for curricula for slow learners is its relevance to the importance of skill learning. Nevertheless, it would be foolish to argue that the only objectives of education for slow learners consist of behaviours which can be observed and measured or assessed, and the objectives curriculum has been criticized as restrictive, narrow, rigid and dangerous (Stenhouse; Hogben).[60] Wheeler's model allows for some flexibility in his concept of 'proximate objectives', or the idea that definitions of objectives are the best possible at the times they are formulated but remain always open to revision in the light of knowledge, experience and the process of evaluation. But more is required. Eisner[61] introduces the idea of 'educational process' involving 'expressive objectives' which emerge in the process. These complement behavioural objectives with situations specifically designed to engage children in a problem or task without specifying in advance what the particular learning outcomes might be. Kerr[62] also extends the objectives model in two main ways. First, he develops curriculum process dimensions complementary to the stages of the objectives model through which he allows for continuous interaction and evaluation between all stages. Secondly, he is specific about the *sources* of the curriculum as:

pupils – the level of their development, needs and interest

society – the social conditions and problems which children are likely to encounter

disciplines – the nature of subject-matter and the types of learning possible from it.

What these writers are seeking to define, and what every efficient, practical teacher will have experienced, is *the objective which emerges in the teaching*. It is a humbling experience to realize that an objective, valuable for the pupils and not planned for, has emerged from a teaching situation. When it emerges as a result of insight or sensitivity on the part of a slow-learning pupil, then excitement mingles with the humility.

Lawton[63] also sees the curriculum as a process. Interaction of philosophical and sociological considerations, mediated by psychological concepts of learning, sequence, structure, etc., enables learning tasks to be selected from the culture and organized as curriculum in teaching stages. Practical considerations of resources, equipment, staffing and so on, intervene at this level and the pressures are to be contained and balanced through the instrument of the school timetable. This brief summary does little justice to Lawton's brave attempt to come to terms with some of the difficult problems posed by a common curriculum. The proposed curriculum involves five cores of knowledge: mathematics, physical and biological sciences, humanities and social studies, expressive arts and moral education. *Every* pupil is to reach a minimum level of understanding and experience in these areas, beyond which there will be wide, individual choice by pupils. A module organization is suggested with remedial education (not defined) sharing, with individual interests and private study, twenty out of eighty-five modules per week which are allocated as discretionary time. Lawton draws heavily upon sociological concepts of 'high' and 'low' culture, related to historical social strata in our society, in discussing both the need for, and the problems of, a common curriculum. He makes use of the ideas of the effect of technological and social changes influencing the cultures, and of continuity of curriculum objectives allied to variety of content, learning experiences and teaching methods. He regards the development of individualized timetables as essential to the achievement of a common curriculum.

What is not clear from Lawton's writing is the question of how common the common curriculum is to be. He quotes with approval from Williams [64] the latter's selection of an outline curriculum, which Williams proposes as 'the minimum aim for every *educationally normal child*' (my italics). For teachers of slow learners that is the question. At what point, if any, do the least successful 15 per cent of the school population (in terms of school progress) cease to be *educationally normal*? And, even if some are to be so regarded, who is to say that they cannot have some area of common curriculum with their fellows – even if it must be the area of awareness rather than understanding? Perhaps the discussion should conclude by repeating the quotation from Hirst [65] in relation to the common curriculum: '[there are] no adequate grounds for saying this is impossible when we have in fact spent so little of our effort trying to achieve this'.

References

1. J. M. C. ITARD, *The Wild Boy of Aveyron.* 1801. Trans. G. and M. Humphrey, Appleton-Century-Crofts, New York, 1932. E. SEGUIN, *Idiocy and its Treatment by the Physiological Method.* 1866. Teachers College Press, Columbia University, New York, 1907.
2. T. S. BALL, *Itard, Seguin and Kephart. Sensory Education, a Learning Interpretation.* Merrill, Columbus, Ohio, 1971.

3. S. A. KIRK and G. O. JOHNSON, *Educating the Retarded Child.*
   Houghton Mifflin, Boston, Mass., 1951.
4. W. K. BRENNAN, *Shaping the Education of Slow Learners.* Routledge
   & Kegan Paul, 1974.
5. M. MONTESSORI, *The Montessori Method,* trans. A. E. George, 1912.
   Schocken, New York, 1972. A. DESCOEUDRES, *The Education of
   Mentally Defective Children.* Harrap, 1928. ITARD, *The Wild Boy of
   Aveyron.* SEGUIN, *Idiocy and its Treatment by the Physiological Method.*
6. A. D. INSKEEP, *Teaching Dull and Retarded Children.* Macmillan,
   1926. P. A. BARON, *Backwardness in Schools.* Blackie, 1938. M. E.
   HILL, *The Education of Backward Children.* Harrap, 1939. Cheshire
   Education Committee, *The Education of Dull Children at the Primary
   Stage.* Hodder & Stoughton Educational, Dunton Green, 1956.
   Cheshire Education Committee, *The Education of Dull Children at
   the Secondary Stage.* Hodder & Stoughton Educational, Dunton
   Green, 1963.
7. J. DUNCAN, *The Education of the Ordinary Child.* Nelson, 1942.
8. R. H. HUNGERFORD, C. J. DEPRUSO and L. E. ROSSENZWEIG,
   'The non-academic pupil', in R. H. Hungerford (ed.), *Philosophy of
   Special Education.* New York Association for Teachers of Special
   Education, 1948. H. GOLDSTEIN and D. SEGAL, *A Curriculum Guide
   for Teachers of Educable Mentally Handicapped.* Department of
   Public Instruction, Springfield, Illinois, 1958.
9. E. H. MARTENS, *Curriculum Adjustment for the Mentally Retarded.*
   Government Printing Office, Washington D.C., rev. edn, 1950.
   W. B. FEATHERSTONE, *Teaching the Slow Learner.* Teachers College
   Press, Columbia University, New York, 1951. C. P. INGRAM, *Education of the Slow Learning Child.* Ronald Press, Oxford, 3rd edn,
   1960.
10. KIRK and JOHNSON, *Educating the Retarded Child.* A. E. TANSLEY
    and R. GULLIFORD, *The Education of Slow Learning Children.*
    Routledge & Kegan Paul, 1960. S. S. SEGAL, *Teaching Backward
    Pupils.* Evans, 1963. Department of Education and Science, *Half
    Our Future* (Newsom Report). HMSO, 1963. Schools Council,
    *Raising the School Leaving Age: a Co-operative Programme of
    Research and Development* (Working Paper No. 2). HMSO, 1965.
    P. BELL, *Basic Teaching for Slow Learners.* Muller, 1970. A. A.
    WILLIAMS, *Basic Subjects for the Slow Learners.* Methuen Educa-
    tional, 1970.
11. A. A. STRAUSS and L. E. LEHTINEN, *Psychopathology and Education
    of Brain Injured Children,* Vol. I. Grune & Stratton, New York,

1947. A. E. TANSLEY, *Reading and Remedial Reading*. Routledge & Kegan Paul, 1967. S. D. BENYON, *Intensive Programming for Slow Learners*. Merrill, Columbus, Ohio, 1968. C. CHANEY and N. C. KEPHART, *Motoric Aids to Perceptual Training*. Merrill, Columbus, Ohio, 1968. M. FROSTIG and P. MASLOW, *Learning Problems in the Classroom*. Grune & Stratton, New York, 1973. W. K. BRENNAN, J. M. JACKSON and J. REEVE, *'Look' Visual Perceptual Materials Handbook*. Macmillan Education, 1972. J. MCCREESH and A. MAHER, *Remedial Education: Objectives and Techniques*. Ward Lock Educational, 1974.

12. KIRK and JOHNSON, *Educating the Retarded Child*.

13. J. E. W. WALLIN, *Education of Mentally Handicapped Children*. Harrap, 1955, chapters 9 and 10.

14. G. D. STEVENS, 'An analysis of objectives for the education of children with retarded mental development', *American Journal of Mental Deficiency*, **63**, 1958, 225–35.

15. G. O. JOHNSON, 'The education of the mentally retarded', in W. M. Cruickshank and G. O. Johnson (eds), *Education of Exceptional Children and Youth*. Staples Press, 1968.

16. Department of Education and Science, *Slow Learners at School*. HMSO, 1964.

17. R. GULLIFORD, *Special Educational Needs*. Routledge & Kegan Paul, 1971.

18. BRENNAN, *Shaping the Education of Slow Learners*.

19. P. H. TAYLOR, *Curriculum Planning for Compensatory Education: a Suggested Procedure*. SC Pamphlet 5. Schools Council, 1970 (out of print).

20. GULLIFORD, *Special Educational Needs*.

21. MCCREESH and MAHER, *Remedial Education: Objectives and Techniques*.

22. BRENNAN, *Shaping the Education of Slow Learners*.

23. J. GARDNER, *Can we be Equal and Excellent too?* Harper & Row, New York, 1961.

24. J. P. WHITE, *Towards a Compulsory Curriculum*. Routledge & Kegan Paul, 1973.

25. W. TAYLOR, *The Secondary Modern School*. Faber, 1964.

26. Ministry of Education, *Education of the Adolescent* (Hadow Report). HMSO, 1926.

27. G. H. BANTOCK, *The Implications of Literacy*. Leicester University Press, 1966. *Culture, Industrialization and Society*. Routledge & Kegan Paul, 1968. 'Towards a theory of popular education', in R. Hooper (ed.), *The Curriculum*. Oliver & Boyd, Edinburgh, 1971.

28. D. HOLBROOK, *English for the Rejected*. Cambridge University Press, 1964.

29. P. H. HIRST, 'Liberal education and the nature of knowledge', in R. D. Archambault (ed.), *Philosophical Analysis and Education*. Routledge & Kegan Paul, 1965. 'The logic of the curriculum', *Journal of Curriculum Studies*, 1, 1969, 142–58.

30. P. H. HIRST and R. S. PETERS, *The Logic of Education*. Routledge & Kegan Paul, 1970.

31. Schools Council, *The Educational Implications of Social and Economic Change* (Working Paper No. 12). HMSO, 1967.

32. HIRST, 'The logic of the curriculum'.

33. HIRST, 'The logic of the curriculum'.

34. M. SHIPMAN, 'Curriculum for inequality?', in R. Hooper (ed.), *The Curriculum*.

35. Department of Education and Science, *Half our Future* (Newsom Report).

36. D. LAWTON, 'Preparation for changes in the curriculum', in J. W. Tibble (ed.), *The Extra Year*. Routledge & Kegan Paul, 1970.

37. Schools Council, *Raising the School Leaving Age* (Working Paper No. 2). HMSO, 1965.

38. DUNCAN, *The Education of the Ordinary Child*.

39. W. P. ALEXANDER, 'Intelligence concrete and abstract', Monograph 19, *British Journal of Psychology*, 1935.

40. KIRK and JOHNSON, *Educating the Retarded Child*. TANSLEY and GULLIFORD, *The Education of Slow Learning Children*. BRENNAN, *Shaping the Education of Slow Learners*.

41. N. C. KEPHART, *The Slow Learner in the Classroom*. Merrill, Columbus, Ohio, 2nd edn, 1971.

42. CHANEY and KEPHART, *Motoric Aids to Perceptual Training*.

43. M. FROSTIG and D. HORNE, *Handbook to the Frostig Programme for the Development of Visual Perception*. Follett, Chicago, 1967.

44. TANSLEY, *Reading and Remedial Reading*.

45. BRENNAN, JACKSON and REEVE, *'Look' Visual Perceptual Materials Handbook*.

46. J. S. BRUNER, *The Process of Education*. Harvard University Press, Cambridge, Mass., 1960.

47. TANSLEY and GULLIFORD, *The Education of Slow Learning Children*.

48. BRENNAN, *Shaping the Education of Slow Learners*.

49. J. J. SCHWAB, 'The practical: a language for the curriculum', *School Review*, **78**, 1969, 1–23. Reprinted in P. H. Taylor and K. A. Tye (eds), *Curriculum, School and Society: an Introduction to*

Curriculum Studies. NFER Publishing, Windsor, 1975.

50. STEVENS, 'An analysis of objectives for the education of children with retarded mental development'.

51. M. F. CLEUGH, *Teaching the Slow Learner.* 3 Vols. Methuen, 1961; SEGAL, *Teaching Backward Pupils*; BELL, *Basic Teaching for Slow Learners*; A. A. WILLIAMS, *Basic Subjects for Slow Learners.*

52. HIRST, 'The logic of the curriculum'.

53. KEPHART, *The Slow Learner in the Classroom.*

54. D. O. HEBB, *The Organization of Behaviour.* John Wiley, New York, 1949.

55. H. F. HARLOW, 'The formation of learning sets', *Psychological Review.* **56**, 1949, 51–65

56. B. S. BLOOM (ed.), *Taxonomy of Educational Objectives: the Classification of Educational Goals.* Handbook I: Cognitive Domain. Longmans Green, 1956. D. R. KRATHWOHL, B. S. BLOOM and B. B. MASIA, *Taxonomy of Educational Objectives: the Classification of Educational Goals.* Handbook II: Affective Domain. Longmans Green, 1964.

57. D. K. WHEELER, *Curriculum Process.* Hodder & Stoughton Educational, Dunton Green, 1967.

58. R. W. TYLER, *Basic Principles of Curriculum and Instruction.* University of Chicago Press, Chicago, 1950. 'Curriculum organisation', in *The Integration of Educational Experience* (National Society for the Study of Education 57th Year Book). University of Chicago Press, Chicago, 1958.

59. H. TABA, *Curriculum Development: Theory and Practice.* Harcourt Brace Jovanovich, New York, 1962.

60. L. STENHOUSE, 'Some limitations on the use of objectives in the curriculum', *Paedagocica Europaea*, 1971, 78–83. *An Introduction to Curriculum Development.* Heinemann Educational Books, 1975. D. HOGBEN, 'The behavioural objectives approach: some problems and dangers', *Journal of Curriculum Studies*, **4**, 1972, 42–50.

61. E. W. EISNER, 'Instructional and expressive educational objectives: their formulation and use in the curriculum', in W. J. Popham (ed.), 'Instructional objectives', AERA Monograph 3. Rand McNally, Chicago, 1969.

62. J. F. KERR, *Changing the Curriculum.* Hodder & Stoughton Educational, Dunton Green, 1968.

63. D. LAWTON, *Social Change, Educational Theory and Curriculum Planning.* Hodder & Stoughton Educational, Dunton Green, 1975.

64. R. WILLIAMS, *The Long Revolution.* Penguin Books, 1961.

65. HIRST, 'The logic of the curriculum'.

IV. Background to the work of the teachers

Introduction

Teachers do not work in a vacuum. They are part of a system of education which interacts with other social systems, defines certain roles for its main institutions, the schools, and in doing so also defines roles for the pupils, teachers, and governors and managers who form the schools. Like other systems and institutions, the education system and the schools are subject to change, which also affects the individuals who operate the system and the schools. Teachers, therefore, work within prescribed limits. But the limits are not always clearly defined and their pattern itself is continually changing and developing.

The social forces which affect teachers and schools have been examined and reviewed in the literature. Jackson and Marsden[1] and Floud et al.[2] have examined the influence of social class; Halsey et al.[3] document interactions between education, economic and social forces; Maclure[4] studies control in education and Baron and Howell,[5] school management and government; Musgrove[6] analyses patterns of power and authority in English education; Taylor et al.[7] look at power, but also at purpose and constraint in primary schools; Keddie[8] brings the analysis closer to the classroom while Musgrove and Taylor[9] examine the role of the teacher as shaped and influenced by social forces, and Lawton[10] relates social change to the curriculum.

It is not the purpose of this chapter to review the above literature, but to outline some of the problems, anxieties and difficulties which have been identified in the course of discussion with teachers of slow learners about the curriculum in their schools, its development and their attitude to it. Professional teachers may find little that is new in this chapter, but the knowledge that their anxieties are shared by colleagues may be helpful in their personal assessments. Readers who are not teachers may be made aware of the complexity of the pressures which affect the concerned teacher in his daily work, and those who would judge the teachers should take account of the complexities they face, especially in the interpretation of any actual or implied criticisms in this report.

Responsibility for the curriculum

It is not easy to identify the source of responsibility for the curriculum in the educational system of England and Wales. Successive secretaries of state for education have consistently indicated that detailed responsibility for the curriculum does not rest with them or with their department. Concern and interest are there, with suggestions carefully propagated through pamphlets, circulars, conferences and the work of Her Majesty's Inspectorate; but authority is firmly rejected. All this is consistent with the current Education Act (1944), which requires only that education is provided which is appropriate to the age, aptitude and ability of the pupil, and that he shall have religious education and experience of corporate worship in school. The Act establishes a shared responsibility between central government and the local education authority, for the provision and management of a national system of education. Is it, then, the LEA which is responsible for the curriculum? There was no information available to the project which suggested that any LEA imposed, or sought to impose, on project schools any edicts or conditions relating to the curriculum. Though relationships between LEAs and the schools were closer, LEA attitudes reflected those of central government described above. Questionnaires completed for the project by assistant education officers for special education reflected similar attitudes. The main concerns of education officers at local level were about the quality of the curriculum in schools; a desire for relevant development; willingness to finance local courses on curriculum development; frustration when financial limitations inhibited development; some belief that the Department of Education and Science should act more positively towards finance and the promotion of curriculum development. Not a single claim, explicitly or implicitly, was made for control over the curriculum of the schools.

All LEAs establish management bodies for their schools, some for individual schools, others on a group basis. In the project schools most LEAs implicitly, and some explicitly, charged the governors or managers of schools with responsibility for the organization, management and curriculum of their schools. However, the common practice was to require the governors or managers to discharge their duties 'in consultation with the headteacher of the school', or words to that effect. This appears to create an ambiguous situation. Governors have responsibility but must share it with the headteacher – between them, where *does* the responsibility reside? In the project schools the difficulty was generally ignored. So far as could be ascertained in discussion, managers or governors rarely did anything positive about the curriculum unless invited to do so by the headteacher, and generally restricted themselves to expressions of interest or concern.

There can be no doubt that headteachers are responsible for the curriculum of their schools, and in the project schools they appeared to accept this responsibility without question. They differed in the degree to which they allowed or encouraged staff involvement in curricular matters, and there was equal variation in the degree to which the responsibility was delegated to members of staff (very extensive in large secondary schools). Nevertheless the ultimate responsibility of the headteacher remained unquestioned. But to whom is the headteacher accountable? There did not appear to be a clear answer to this question. Headteachers have the ambiguity of responsibility shared with governors or managers who may raise questions about the curriculum, as may local inspectors or HMI, and any of these may involve the headteacher in general discussion of the school curriculum. But there did not appear to be any clear authority whereby the headteacher could be required to take specific action in relation to the curriculum of the school. It does appear, therefore, that a very high degree of responsibility for the school curriculum rests with the headteacher, though, because of the circumstances and traditions of the educational system, the responsibility is not accompanied by clear accountability.

The legal rights of parents in relation to schools are confined to their own children and centre on the choice of school, itself limited by practical circumstances. Bodies of parents appear to have no legal rights. In many project schools there were parent–teacher associations, though questions of curriculum tended to be excluded by the constitution of these associations. In practice there is usually discussion and explanation, but few heads would brook direct interference from this source. In some LEAs there were parent representatives on governing or managing bodies, but they, too, were subject to the limitations and ambiguities discussed above.

There can be no denial of the fact that communities should have a vital interest in the education of their young. If so, how is the interest expressed? A short answer is: 'not very well'. The avenue of influence is through elected members of local councils who are members of the education committee or on managing or governing bodies of local schools. It has been shown above how limited and ambiguous both these bodies are in relation to the school curriculum. Of course there are indirect means by which the community (or parents) may influence curriculum. In newspapers, television and radio discussions, and in public meetings, questions are continually being asked and criticisms ventilated about schools, their curricula and the quality of their teaching; and these questions are often raised by MPs in Parliament.

Historical reasons for the current situation

The purpose of the above discussion is to emphasize that responsibility for the curriculum is not clearly defined in the contemporary educational system. This situation appears to be the result of the way government has evolved which has led to a division of power between central and local govenment or, more positively, to their co-operation in the provision and management of a national system of education. Additionally, British suspicion of central power, allied to a belief that education, or at least its content, should be safeguarded from direct political intervention from whatever source, has effectively prevented the emergence of centralized curricula or curricular control. Similar beliefs appear to have operated at local level and have protected the independence of the schools in curricular matters. There has also been a widespread belief that in education, which depends upon complex relationships between the taught and those who teach them, curricular responsibility *should* be within the school where pupils' needs can be identified and action to satisfy them initiated in a speedy, relevant and efficient manner. Though there are exceptions to this principle (particularly in terms of public examinations), the result has been a system shared between government, LEAs and schools which has achieved remarkable and exceptional flexibility and a strength and quality which rests on very considerable but relevant variety among the schools in the system.

It could also be argued that the decentralized strength of the present system is the result of its evolution in times more settled than our own. Though the development was in response to social change, that change itself rested on moral values more certain than today's, upon more settled political and economic objectives, upon greater certainty about the role and strength of Britain in the world, and even upon more certainty about the knowledge and skills required by the young if they were to participate in and contribute to the community in which they would be adults.

General difficulties in the current situation

The above certainties are no longer a main feature of society in the present phase of rapid social and economic changes. Not only new social mores, but new nations, new industrial techniques, new means of communication, new relationships between the sexes and between generations, as well as unexpected and unprecedented inflation, have contributed to change at a pace which generates considerable anxiety about the future. In these circumstances social cohesion and the maintenance of traditional values and relationships have ever greater attraction for some people, while others see tradition as an obstacle which makes more difficult the changes required if desirable values are to be expressed and communicated in ways suited to contemporary conditions and calculated to secure their survival in a form consistent with a changed future. As schools both transmit the culture and contribute to its modification, both the above groups find things to criticize in the work of schools, thus subjecting the teachers to powerful, contradictory pressures. But the teachers are subjected to the same doubts and uncertainties and themselves divide between the groups. So the pressures are not only *on* the schools – they are *in* the schools. There they may influence teachers' beliefs and actions on questions of curriculum. One result of this is that teachers often appear to lack confidence in their professional role and to some degree they may have lost the confidence of troubled parents and a troubled community faced with contradictory opinions from the professionals to whom they look for advice and guidance.

In project schools the uncertainty was expressed in a variety of ways. Criticism of parents and/or of 'modern youth'; unwillingness to take a positive view of school organization, curriculum or teaching method; distortion of 'child-centred' philosophies of education which appeared to remove responsibility from teachers; doubt about the role of the school and, in the extreme, rejection of any role for the school – these and similar attitudes appeared to reflect the basic anxiety and uncertainty.

Professional difficulties in the current situation

In addition to the ambiguities of the system of education and the general uncertainties which teachers share with parents and other members of the community, teachers are subjected to special pressures which originate within their profession. Their own professional frame of reference is itself unstable and fluctuating. Moreover, the changes of 'fashion' appear to take place well within the length of service of individual teachers. One result is that the more calm (or the more cynical) teachers in project schools were concerned that, if only they remained unchanging in their ways, 'fashion' would turn the complete circle and they would be professionally up to date again!

Some examples illustrate the above statement. Part of the folklore of teaching is the era of 'standards', interacting as it did with 'payment by results'. Eventually this was followed by an era of 'child-centred' education. The first period, limited though it was, focused upon what pupils *could do*; the second, in its extreme, shifted the focus to what children *were*. It may well be that the current interest in behavioural objectives goes at least some of the way back to an earlier concern with standards of achievement. There have been changes in fashions of teaching reading, in the fluctuation of alphabetic, phonic, look-and-say, sentence or experience methods, and continuing debate about i.t.a., as well as changes in organization from class programmes through group reading to individualized reading. Learning based upon duty, discipline and even fear has given way to learning based upon interest, involvement and participation on the part of the pupil. The teacher has moved from being an unquestioned source of knowledge to the 'shaper' guiding the learning of the pupil, after passing through a period in which he appeared to place all the responsibility for learning on to his immature pupils.

The period between the two world wars saw 'progressive' educationists advocating the introduction of streaming as necessary to make the teaching of all pupils effective, but particularly to make sure that disadvantaged, under-privileged pupils received equitable attention from the teacher. Today, 'progressive' teachers campaign for the ending of streaming or segregation and its replacement by mixed-ability teaching, stating a case almost identical to that which, forty years ago, was used to support streaming. Maybe there is now another swing under way, for some of the banding seen in project schools was little different from earlier streaming! Finally, there is the recent stress on what is called 'structured learning', which is held by some teachers to have special benefit for slow learners. To many older teachers this appears like a return to formal teaching methods in which, they say, they were trained, but which they abandoned, usually under pressure from above. Faced with all this, it is not surprising that many older teachers in the second half of their service find it difficult either to accommodate to the contemporary situation or to maintain a stable professional position.

Miel[11] suggested that these educational movements fall into three major theoretical patterns: the *linear*, where what is left is never returned to; the *pendulum*, which goes from one side to the other, leaving everyone confused or attempting to anticipate the change in direction; and the *spiral,* where there is change due to experience, experiment or even fashion, but where each return to a situation is subtly different as a result of experience – and particularly experience of its opposite. The first position is simple and uncritical, the second cynical and the third most rational, suggesting that though history may repeat itself it will be experienced differently the second time round. There appear also to be swings between the three explanations of movement in educational theory and practice.

Special difficulties for teachers of slow learners

Teachers of slow learners are influenced by all the general and professional difficulties described above but their role also exposes them to certain special difficulties. The factors creating the difficulties may be illustrated by reference to intelligence, attainment, curriculum and teaching organization. Though these factors affect all teachers, they have special importance for teachers of slow learners.

INTELLIGENCE

The intelligence factor concerns the shifts between the view of intelligence as genetically determined and unchangeable and the view that it is the result of environment and experience: 'nature versus nurture'. Hunt[12] has listed six changed or changing beliefs affected by the shifts (stated in pre-changed form):

1   A belief in fixed intelligence
2   A belief in predetermined development
3   A belief in a fixed, static, switchboard nature of brain function
4   A belief that early, pre-speech development is unimportant
5   A belief that if experience affects later development it is through the effect of emotional reactions or instinctual needs
6   A belief that learning must be motivated by homeostatic need, painful stimulation, or by acquired drives based upon these.

These changing beliefs affect not only the teacher's view of the slow learner and his abilities, but also the teacher's concept of the value of intelligence tests and their role and limitations in the classroom. To add to the teacher's confusion, there is not universal agreement about the changes.[13]

ATTAINMENT

The teacher's views of attainment tests have also been influenced by the factors noted in the previous paragraph. The concept of under-achievement, for instance, which long held sway, depended upon relating the results of attainment tests to those from intelligence tests, a simplistic rélationship no longer tenable. Added to this, the tendency of psychologists to move away from 'normative' tests towards greater reliance on 'criterion'-based assessment has introduced another change in the classroom. Meanwhile changes in curricula and teaching methods, especially in mathematics, have made tests in this area prematurely obsolescent. The so-called diagnostic tests are also affected by these changes. The idea that the Schonell[14] or Daniels and Diack[15] diagnostic tests will 'explain' a pupil's failures is fading. Recent skill-analysis approaches show these tests as attainment tests in the sub-skills which support higher-order skills. As such the tests provide valuable information about the pupil's performance, but they do not indicate, for instance, whether the pupil's failure in phonics is the result of a learning difficulty or is simply because he has not been properly taught. More than ever this kind of interpretation is seen to depend on the information, insight and skill possessed by the teacher. This view enhances the importance of the teacher's role, but it also generates anxiety. Some of the best teachers in project schools welcomed the change of emphasis but doubted if their training and experience had equipped them for the enhanced role.

CURRICULUM

The effect of curriculum changes on tests has been noted, but they also affect teaching methods, concepts of standards and techniques of assessment. Fluctuations and differences also occur in basic thinking about curriculum for slow learners exemplified by the review of the literature and the debate about a common or separate curriculum noted in the previous chapter. The basic move from learning as reproduction of facts to learning involving insight, understanding and generalization, which has had a considerable effect on the curriculum, is also of concern to teachers of pupils who have difficulties in both areas of learning.

ORGANIZATION

Whatever its merits or de-merits, the recent trend towards mixed-ability organization has important consequences for teachers of slow learners. In some project schools formerly well-established classes or departments for slow learners had ceased to exist. The teachers had lost their somewhat separate and distinct role and were struggling to develop a new role – in most schools as a teacher of a mixed-ability class with additional vaguely defined responsibility for slow learners; in one, as a full-time adviser working with and through colleagues in mixed-ability groups. Other teachers of slow learners were involved in team teaching, attempting to 'feed in' their knowledge and experience of slow learners tȯ a new situation. Schools were observed in which the teachers of slow learners seemed particularly troubled in adjusting and contributing to the new situations, often because the situations themselves failed to provide the teachers with the satisfactions which had previously motivated them, while new satisfactions had not yet emerged. Some teachers appeared to lack the flexibility or personality attributes required in their more complex, emerging roles.

The new situations are demanding. They are new to most teachers, especially in secondary schools. Class or subject teachers are overwhelmed by the problems of making their own contributions effective in the new conditions; they tend to relegate the problem of the minority of slow learners to second place and this is resented by colleagues who must advise on the needs of such pupils.

Summary

It can be seen, therefore, that teachers are affected, like all members of society, by the rapid pace of contemporary economic, social and cultural change. The contradictory pressures generated do not just bear *on* the school, they are *in* the schools as teachers respond differently to the pressures, assuming different attitudes to curriculum, teaching method and school organization. It is also clear that teachers are further confused by changes in curriculum, method and organization, both theoretically and in practice. Some of these changes bear special consequences for teachers of slow learners, especially those relating to the nature of intelligence, concepts of attainment and standards, the general curriculum and the move to mixed-ability organization.

All the above circumstances create uncertainty in schools and generate anxiety among teachers. Teachers of slow learners are in a particularly demanding situation which should be taken into account in any evaluation of their work.

References

1. B. JACKSON and D. MARSDEN, *Education and the Working Class.* Routledge & Kegan Paul, 1962.
2. E. FLOUD, A. H. HALSEY and E. M. MARTIN, *Social Class and Educational Opportunity.* Heinemann, 1956.

3. A. H. HALSEY, J. FLOUD and C. A. ANDERSON, *Education, Economy and Society*. Free Press, New York, 1961.

4. S. MACLURE, 'The control of education', in History of Education Society, *Studies in the Government and Control of Education since 1860*. Methuen, 1970.

5. G. BARON and D. A. HOWELL, *School Management and Government*. HMSO, 1968.

6. F. MUSGROVE, *Patterns of Power and Authority in English Education*. Methuen, 1971.

7. P. H. TAYLOR, W. A. REID, B. J. HOLLEY and GAIL EXON, *Purpose, Power and Constraint in the Primary School Curriculum*. Schools Council Research Studies. Macmillan Education, 1974.

8. N. KEDDIE, 'Classroom Knowledge', in M.F.D. Young (ed.), *Knowledge and Control: New Directions in the Sociology of Education*. Collier Macmillan, 1971.

9. F. MUSGROVE and P. H. TAYLOR, *Society and the Teacher's Role*. Routledge & Kegan Paul, 1969.

10. D. LAWTON, *Social Change, Educational Theory and Curriculum Planning*. Hodder & Stoughton Educational, Dunton Green, 1975.

11. A. MIEL, 'Reassessment of curriculum – why?', in D. Huebner (ed.), *A Reassessment of the Curriculum*. Teachers College Press, Columbia University, New York, 1964.

12. J. MCV. HUNT, *Intelligence and Experience*. Ronald Press, Oxford, 1961. 'Environment, development and scholastic experience', in M. Deutsch, I. Katz and A. R. Jensen (eds), *Social Class, Race and Psychological Development*. Holt, Rinehart & Winston, 1968. Reprinted in H. J. Butcher and D. E. Lomax (eds), *Readings in Human Intelligence*. Methuen, 1972.

13. A. R. JENSEN, 'How much can we boost IQ and scholastic achievement?', *Harvard Educational Review*, **39**, 1969, 1–123.

14. F. J. SCHONELL and F. E. SCHONELL, *Diagnostic and Attainment Testing*. Oliver & Boyd, Edinburgh, 1963.

15. J. C. DANIELS and H. DIACK, *The Standard Reading Tests*. Chatto & Windus, 1969.

V. The shape of the curriculum in the schools

Introduction

There are two main sources for the information which is classified, generalized and presented in this chapter: the curricular documents made available to the project by the project schools and the oral and written reports of project members who visited the schools, discussed the curriculum with teachers, and observed the quality of work in teaching situations. Other, supplementary, sources of information, of great value to the interpretation of the material from schools, were:

1 Reports of discussions by working parties of teachers established in teachers' centres
2 Reports of discussions held by experienced teachers following advanced courses in special education
3 Reports from working parties organized by the associations of teachers in remedial and special education
4 Contributions from associations of subject teachers
5 Written contributions from individual teachers.

Less specific, but still valuable were the many points made in discussion following the conferences, courses and meetings attended by project members in many parts of England and Wales.

One reaction to the above list might be to allege that the information is subjective. So it is; but the subjectivity originates from many different sources and cannot be held to be unduly influenced by any particular groups or opinions. Another answer would be to point out that almost the whole subject of the curriculum is subjective, that a 'science' of the curriculum has yet to be formulated, and that as a large part of curriculum thinking is concerned with values and the priorities which should emerge from them, the 'science' may be a long time in coming. Indeed, it may never be appropriate to the whole discussion of curriculum, though this should not discourage the search for objectivity in those parts of the curriculum where this is appropriate and possible.

Another reaction might well be that the generalizations and inter-pretations which follow are also subjective. So they are. Yet there is a sense in which the generalizations, interpretations and opinions retain some objectivity, because the project team was free from any committed philosophy of the curriculum or theory about its organization at the beginning of the project, and any opinions or conclusions reached, there-fore, have been shaped by the study of the literature and documentation, by observation in schools and by interaction with teachers. In other words, conclusions emerge from the work of the project.

Attitudes to the curriculum in the schools

There was no evidence in the project schools that any LEA had developed any consistent attitude or policy about the detail of curricula in its schools, and no evidence of any agreed or centralized procedure for the recording of curricula or curricular decisions. Nor did any documents submitted from any source raise this as a practice or even as a desirable development. This means that the curriculum in each school is generated, developed and recorded within the particular school. The wide variation in docu-ments from the schools – variation in content, comprehensiveness, format and presentation – confirms this conclusion.

Within the schools a basic attitude concerned the importance attached to the development and recording of a *written* curriculum. Documents on the curriculum (not necessarily comprehensive curricula) were received from 67 per cent of primary, 72 per cent of secondary and 84 per cent of special schools. Thus approximately one in three primary schools, one in four secondary schools and one in six special schools did not supply any written account of curricula. Follow-up visits showed that in the majority of these schools the written record did not exist. It should be noted that the above figures refer to curricula for slow-learning pupils and do not necessarily represent the general situation in the schools. In some ordinary schools well-documented curricula existed in the school generally, or in subject departments, in contrast with its absence in depart-ments for slow learners, while in other schools the situation was reversed. It was difficult to ascertain the reasons for the absence of written curricula. In some schools staff changes were responsible, especially of heads of department; in other schools, pressure on staff, general disorganization, or even unconcern appeared to be influencing the situation, though in all these there was lack of positive insistence by headteachers or senior teachers. There were schools in which these negative attitudes were not operative factors and the absence of recorded curricula appeared to be a deliberate decision arising out of the philosophy subscribed to by the headteacher or the teacher in charge of slow learners. Approximately 15 per cent of primary, 11 per cent of secondary and 7 per cent of special schools had decided that written curricula were undesirable or unsuitable for slow-learning pupils.

A word of caution is necessary about written curricula. It must not be assumed that the absence of a written curriculum necessarily indicates inferior work in a school. Some small special and primary schools, along with some secondary departments, devoted considerable time to discussion of the curriculum and held the view that the intimacy and quality of communication made written curricula unnecessary. There were good, successful schools among these, but the success often rested on the quality of teaching and organization rather than upon the curriculum. It is asking a great deal for any individual teacher or group of teachers to keep in mind all aspects of the curriculum required for the task of arranging regular revision and review. Nor must the converse be uncritically accepted. Well-organized written curricula do not necessarily live up to their promise in action and may be made ineffective by mediocre teaching. An attitude also exists which regards problems as solved once the plan for their solution has been worked out and written down. The attitude to the curriculum in some schools could be so described. Very often this reflected a basic unconcern with evaluation, or even with outcomes as such. About 5 per cent of written curricula had remained unrevised over long periods of time. Allied to this were schools where the written curriculum had been revised but not the practice, so that what was going on in classrooms had only a slight resemblance to what should have been happening according to the documents.

This unsatisfactory situation arises from an attitude which was widely operative in the schools. It appears to be the result of over-concentration on pupil interest or motivation, or perhaps from misinterpretations of the 'child-centred' philosophy, and holds that, because slow learners are difficult to motivate and do not maintain interest for long periods, then the learning situation must constantly shift in response to changing interests or moods of the pupils. It is argued that a written curriculum is therefore superfluous. Unfortunately, this attitude frequently went hand-in-hand with unconcern about the recording of pupils' activities. In these situations, without forecasts or records, the continuity of the pupil's learning was constantly at risk, especially when there was a change of class teacher or a change of class by the pupil.

It would be dangerously easy to argue that, because responsibility for the curriculum so clearly rests within the schools, then responsibility for negative attitudes must also rest within the schools. Before accepting such a simplistic proposition, certain aspects of the schools must be noted. First, unconcern about curriculum does not necessarily imply unconcern about pupils. Concern about pupils, about their present and future welfare was a positive and moving feature of almost all project schools. This was allied to considerable knowledge about the learning difficulties of pupils, both cognitive and motivational, one consequence being a concentration by the teachers on methods of reducing the difficulties for the pupils and on curriculum content to capture and hold their interest. The widespread use of project and topic approaches came directly out of this concern. Concentration of attention in this way was a contributory factor to the relative lack of concern about the detail of curriculum objectives. Secondly, the training of the teachers and the circumstances in which they work do not create attitudes conducive to attention to behavioural aspects of the curriculum. Until recently, colleges and departments of education have treated curriculum mainly in terms of aims, content and method, and it is safe to assume that few teachers in senior positions in schools had any contact in training with approaches to the curriculum which make a point of stressing behavioural objectives. Attitudes in LEAs, among local inspectors and even among HMIs are similar to those in schools, for the personnel involved are from the same background as the teachers. Until recently, therefore, there has been no countervailing pressure in the schools to question the attitude to the curriculum shaped by the training and general experience of the teachers. This is confirmed by information from those schools which gave high priority and commendable consideration to the curriculum. In such schools attention was almost exclusively directed to content, aims and teaching methods with little attention to objectives and, consequently, little effort at evaluation outside the measurement of elementary progress in the basic subjects.

Without attempting to remove responsibility from schools, it may be admitted that responsibility for the weaknesses noted in attitudes to the curriculum is shared by the system of teacher training and the framework of supervision within which the schools operate. Different attitudes are beginning to emerge in both training and supervision, and within the schools themselves. But before any real 'sharpening' of work on the curriculum can become widespread there needs to be considerable modification of attitudes to the curriculum in the schools. There appears to be a role here for LEA in-service training and for school-based courses, as well as for nationally recruited courses. There is evidence that this kind of provision is beginning to emerge.

Curricula in schools: general

The shape of the curricula, as indicated by the documents submitted to the project and by discussion with teachers, followed from and reflected the attitudes discussed in the previous section. Shape was most clearly discernible in curricular documents from special schools and from separate departments or classes for slow learners in secondary or primary schools. Where the organization for slow learners was based on withdrawal from ordinary classes, the shape was less clear, usually because this situation covered only part of the curriculum being followed by the withdrawn pupils. In general, withdrawal teaching was limited to basic subjects, though in some schools there was a limited allocation of time for social studies or humanities. Least clear of all was the curriculum for slow learners participating in mixed-ability classes. In these circumstances it seemed to be generally assumed that the slow learners would follow the curriculum considered suitable for the class as a whole and the documentation was mainly concerned with modifications of teaching *methods* which might be required for slow learners, or with examples of modified follow-up assignments designed with slow learners in mind. The latter was a feature where mixed-ability organization was associated with team teaching, and occurred most frequently in secondary schools.

Somewhere between the separate classes and mixed-ability teaching were the various degrees of setting or banding practised in schools. Where setting in basic subjects was combined with mixed-ability teaching, curriculum shape tended to be at the level of withdrawal teaching, for in this organization the slow learners are in a remarkably similar situation, except that the class from which they have been withdrawn has temporarily disintegrated. In the sets for slow learners the shape of the curriculum was usually modified by a reduction of content to allow for the assumed slower progress of the pupils. Banding generated a different curriculum pattern. It extended over wider areas of the curriculum than setting, created classes that were together for longer periods, and appeared closely connected with resolving timetable problems, which may have accounted for its appearance in large secondary schools. In practice, and so far as the bands occupied by slow learners were concerned, the organization came very close to the older type of streamed situation. One advantage of this was that it created a situation in which the banded classes could have had substantial periods of time with a class teacher: in practice the opportunity was rarely exploited. The curricula of the 'lower' or more restricted bands were frequently shaped by the dropping of curricular areas, such as a second language, the restriction of laboratory work in science and the reduction of time allotted for more advanced mathematical studies. Subject areas retained were less academic, more utilitarian and more outgoing than in the 'higher' or academic bands. Usually more time was allocated to the elementary skills in basic subjects and humanities/social studies tended to be organized as broad subject areas.

In the separate departments for slow learners, and in special schools, the curriculum shape had many of the features noted for the more restricted bands. But there were important differences. More time was spent with class teachers; there was more work linking school and neighbourhood; skills in basic subjects were better exploited in other areas of curricula; social and personal development was given more attention as part of the curriculum; and recording and continuity were usually arranged in a more positive manner. In these aspects the curriculum in separate classes for slow learners and in special schools was more appropriate than in the other types of organization. The price paid for this was segregation, which had some adverse effects on the curriculum by reducing the exposure of slow learners to the stimulation of their normal peers and to teaching by specialist teachers at the secondary level. Both these could have negative effects on the pupils' aspirations and may have restricted, indirectly, their teachers' expectations of their pupils, thus in a subtle manner tending to restrict the curriculum unnecessarily. Conversely, in certain secondary schools, the exposure of slow-learning pupils to appropriate and well-organized specialist teaching by subject teachers had a positive effect on the pupils' attitudes to learning, improving their motivation and desire to learn. Even more important, these positive benefits did not seem to be confined to the individual subject sessions but appeared to be carried over to learning in the general work of the separate slow-learners' classes. The extent and quality of this kind of interaction in the curriculum for slow learners varied between the schools, but it should be noted that no situations were observed in which a slow-learners' class was totally separated from contact with the general teaching going on in the ordinary school. This kind of stimulation is more difficult to arrange in the curriculum of the special school, though there are signs that teachers are aware of the danger of their isolation and are taking steps to combat it. There are a growing number of linked courses with colleges of further education which offer not only areas of curriculum new to the special-school pupils but also new levels of stimulation and aspiration in subject areas which they have previously experienced in their own schools. These developments should be encouraged and widened by the participation of more schools and colleges, but they require extension in another way. Most of the linked courses observed take place in the final, or the penultimate and final year of statutory education. Many special-school pupils would benefit from earlier stimulation of this kind, when they may be too young or immature to link with the normal activities of the further education college, and when their presence in the college would stretch the bounds of legality. Why not organize some linking of special schools with comprehensive schools, balanced perhaps by the contribution of special-school teachers to work with the slow learners *in* the comprehensive school and some contribution by secondary-school specialist subject teachers in the curriculum of the special school? Moves like this would extend curricula and break down the invisible barrier which separates the special schools from the ordinary schools.

Whatever the source of curriculum documents, some common points were very impressive. First, the accuracy of detail with which the life situations of slow learners were described; secondly, the comprehensive accounts of the common causative factors contributing to their learning difficulties; and thirdly, the descriptions of the characteristics of the slow learners for whom the curriculum was intended.

The outcome of the general discussion is to emphasize that:

1 Curriculum and organization interact, with some evidence that the latter unduly influences the former
2 Different organizations may have features in common which lead to similarities in curriculum shape
3 Separation of slow learners appears to promote more positive and appropriate curriculum shape
4 At the same time separation reduces the stimulation and may adversely affect the aspiration level of pupils and the expectation of teachers
5 Interaction with normal pupils and subject teachers appears to reduce the effect of 4 in ordinary schools
6 Linked courses offer similar opportunities for special schools.

It is noted especially that concentration on content, aims and method has a limiting effect upon curricular shape.

Curricula in schools: specific shape

The manner in which the schools concentrate on content, aims and methods, in that order of importance, has been noted above. In this section these and other aspects of the curriculum will be commented on in more detail.

AIMS IN THE CURRICULUM

Though aims did not take precedence over content in the curricula of the schools, they were generally well stated. In their philosophical approach to curricula most teachers seem aware of the need to enrich the life of the individual; to enable the individual to express and enjoy his individuality in society, if possible by contributing to it; and to enable the individual to impose disciplines on himself so that he will act properly towards others. Thus they formulate individual, social, ethical and moral aims. These aims were stated in the curricular submissions in a variety of ways, many excellent and all showing exceptional insight into the needs of slow learners and the educational aims which those needs call for.

In stating aims in the curriculum a common pattern emerged in which the general aims of the curriculum were stated, followed by statements of more specific aims relevant to a particular area of the curriculum, as in the following example:

> The aim in educating slow-learning pupils is to enable the individual to achieve the greatest possible individual richness, to learn to express that richness in ways acceptable to the society in which he must live and to ensure that he is capable of achieving the highest possible degree of economic and social independence compatible with his aptitudes and abilities.
> The aim of the English language curriculum is to enable the pupil to use language accurately and flexibly in stating his own needs, intentions or feelings, and to ensure that he is capable of understanding the language of other persons and able to comprehend their needs, intentions and feelings as expressed in language by them. Supplementary to this, the language curriculum will contribute to the pupil's perception and awareness of the richness and variety of his natural, cultural and social environment. In pursuing these aims it will also be the purpose of the language curriculum to contribute to the development of reading skills and extend language in its written form.

This example is representative of the more comprehensive statements of aims in curricula from the schools but it also indicates the general trend of discussion in schools without a written curriculum.

An interesting point about aims in the project schools was that the teachers were not usually aware of the nature of statements of aims and the limitations which follow from that nature. There was not, for instance, acute and continuous awareness that aims stated as above are *not* specific to slow learners and would stand equally well as statements of aims for any or all of the pupils in schools. Nor was there clear understanding that, in a democratic society, such universal application was the test of educational aims and that there was something dubious about aims which failed the test. The fact that parts of statements of aims refer to the *intentions* of the teacher and other parts to pupil *outcomes* was not always clearly understood, and where it was, the understanding that references to pupil outcomes were so general as to be of little value in specifying pupil behaviour did not always follow. Another aspect of aims – that they assume maturity and are, quite properly, concerned with mature individuals subsequent to their formal education – was not always clearly perceived. As a result there was sometimes a lack of awareness of the great gap which exists between the statements of aims and the levels of immaturity and incompetence at which pupils enter the schools. Put another way, this means that in most schools there was a lack of a clear understanding that statements of curricular aims are made in a philosophical–ethical frame of reference and require translation into descriptions of pupil behaviour in a psychological–sociological frame of reference if they are to contribute fully to the work of the schools. This failure is mainly responsible for the neglect of curriculum objectives and for the leap from aims to content which was a main feature of the curricula of the schools.

OBJECTIVES IN THE CURRICULUM

In the review of curriculum literature (Chapter III) there is discussion of the nature of behavioural objectives[1] and of the complementary expressive objectives,[2] while throughout the discussion so far it has been implied that such objectives are not a strong feature of curricula in the project schools. It must be faced that, in those schools, the definition of objectives as the knowledge, skills, attitudes, values, sensitivities, etc., which pupils are expected to achieve as a result of the teaching they receive is not common practice, and this is the weakest part of the curricula. It is not merely that attempts to define objectives are weak or inadequate: in most curricula the attempt is not made. Similarly, though teachers are frequently emphatic in their view that important curricular objectives defy behavioural definition, the specification of critical learning situations from which such expressive or process objectives or values may emerge does not commonly occur in the curriculum documents.

When the question of objectives was brought up in discussion with teachers, some made brave attempts to offer definitions; others made the attempt only in response to direct questioning, and rarely did objectives emerge easily and naturally in discussion of the curriculum. Where objectives are discernible in curricular documents or emerge in discussion with teachers, they are usually in an extremely generalized form. In this form they are almost indistinguishable from those aspects of aims which were noted above as referring to pupil outcomes in the curriculum and, similarly, are of little value for the specification of anticipated pupil behaviour.

Given the common attitude to curriculum discussed earlier, the situation described here is not surprising. Attitudes and practice have similar roots and patterns of causation, and the earlier discussion of contributory factors in the training and experience of teachers is relevant to practice as well as to attitudes. Lack of concern with behavioural objectives allows the uncritical leap from aims to content in curricula; it also reduces the emphasis on the efficiency of recording and evaluation discussed below.

In certain curricular areas, such as home economics, heavy crafts and physical education, there is usually more precise definition of the pupil behaviour expected to be established through the curriculum. In part this is due to the practical nature of the subjects and the primacy of skills, but in the best examples the skills were being used as gateways to insight and concept formation.

CONTENT IN THE CURRICULUM

Specification and description of the content of the curriculum forms the major part of the curriculum documents submitted to the project. There is little variation in this between primary, secondary and special schools, the more competent submissions from all sources being remarkable for the care with which the content has been selected, the detail of its organization and the clarity of its presentation. Any variation seems influenced more by the type of organization than the type of school, the most precise documents emanating from situations where slow learners are segregated in special schools or classes, the documents becoming less precise as the situations change through banding, setting and complete mixed-ability teaching, in that order.

In the organization of content, curricula from all sources indicate that basic subject content is considered separately and there is detailed specification of content for arithmetic/mathematics, English language, reading and written English. Beyond these subjects, primary and special schools organize in terms of broad subject fields or use topic/centre-of-interest organizations. Secondary schools continue the subject organization more widely in other curricular areas but there are indications that, where there are separate departments for slow learners, the pattern in these approximates more closely to that of the primary and special schools.

The content of basic subjects is set out in a traditional manner as material to be taught to pupils by the teacher. In arithmetic, for instance, computational processes and skills are usually ordered in terms of the logic of the subject and allocated for classes or age groups on the basis of increased complexity equating with increasing age. Conceptual content is indicated in early primary curricula and in the 'social' or 'survival' aspects of the curricula in secondary and special schools. Between these extremes concept content is rarely developed except in primary schools following the more modern approach to mathematics. The content of reading curricula is usually stated in a similar manner. The skills and even the vocabulary are organized on the basis of the complexity and age dimensions, frequently detailed in terms of the pages or sections of textbooks to be studied and learned. In both arithmetic and reading, content tends to be established on the principle of an essential minimum of material and skill considered appropriate for the pupils for whom the curriculum is intended.

Broad fields of study, centres of interest or topic organizations, which are predominant outside basic subjects, all involve the collection and integration of information from different traditional subject areas. In curriculum documents the contents are usually listed by subject in a traditional manner, though in the better presentations an attempt is made to provide a structure which suggests teaching sequences calculated to assist the integration of knowledge considered important for the pupil. An example of this is the organization of traditional subject-matter in vertical columns with horizontal rows marking out the content of sub-topics or sub-themes. Stated in this way, the content suggests or implies certain cognitive or conceptual objectives for the pupils in a similar manner to that suggested by Hirst[3] for the traditional subject organization. It could be argued that such objectives emerge from the selection of content and, if there has not been specific consideration of objectives by the teacher, then the content-generated objectives may not match the objectives most required by the slow learner. There is some merit in this point though it should be noted as equally applicable to the traditional subject organizations favoured in the project secondary schools. It will also be recalled, from the review of curriculum literature (page 35), that Hirst contended that topic or similar organizations were selected mainly because they resolved the problem of motivating learning for slow-learning pupils, but that they made the achievements of cognitive objectives more difficult. No doubt he was right in so far as excellent teaching is required at the presentation stage if the positive advantage is to be gained without suffering the disadvantage. Perhaps this is what Hirst meant when he labelled the topic approach difficult to handle in the classroom. However that may be, the topic is certainly easier to handle when all aspects of it are under the control of one teacher. This situation occurs more frequently in the primary and special schools than in the secondary schools; it may be a factor in the persistence of subject organization in the latter schools.

There is little doubt about the efficiency of the integrated type of study in assisting slow learners to establish useful, general concepts, and content organized in this way has much to commend it when well taught. One weakness was noted, however, which received little attention in curriculum documents or in discussion with teachers. It is possible for slow learners taught by integrated methods to establish good, working concepts without being aware of the classification of the concepts established during their studies. At first many teachers did not consider this point to be important. Yet it is of the first importance if one of the objectives of the curriculum is to equip the pupil to be able to continue learning independently, away from or after school. Almost all libraries and other retrieval systems are organized on subject lines. To use the catalogues of these effectively the user must be aware of the nature of the material or concepts which he wishes to follow up, which means that he must be able to place these accurately as history, geography, science, art, etc. The ability to operate in this way has an important bearing on the pupil's achievement of independent learning and is worth attention in the organization and presentation of curriculum content.

In the project schools content is not only the larger part of the curriculum but in the absence of clear thinking about objectives it also becomes a main determinant of them. There appears to be a relationship between the type of organization for slow learners and the selection of curriculum content, which tends to become less precise and possibly less immediately appropriate as organization moves towards full mixed-ability teaching. This is more apparent in relation to skills and concepts than in affective or social content.

Though the above review accurately reflects the general situation in the schools, a special note is required about the content of motor–visual–perceptual curricula being developed in the reception classes and assessment units of some special schools, and in a few primary schools for deprived pupils. These curricula were commonly referred to as 'programmes' by the teachers concerned. Content was very carefully detailed in terms of the sub-skills of the motor–visual–perceptual functions covered in the curricula. The main sources for content were: motor-development programmes (Kephart);[4] visual-perception programmes (Frostig and Horne);[5] remedial programmes (Tansley);[6] and visual–perceptual material (Brennan, Jackson and Reeve).[7] Related to these approaches, and often combined with them, were specific language curricula, usually based upon the *Illinois Test of Psycholinguistic Ability*[8] or the Reynell test.[9] In some situations the close specification of content had been extended to the social competence curriculum, using *Progress Assessment Charts*,[10] *The Vineland Social Maturity Scale*[11] or *The Manchester Scales of Social Adaptation*.[12] Other sources mentioned were the *Bristol Social Adjustment Guides*[13] and *Motor Impairment and Compensatory Education*.[14] Further reference to these curricula is made in *Reading for Slow Learners: a Curriculum Guide*.[15]

METHOD IN THE CURRICULUM

In most curriculum submissions methods developed from consideration of the circumstances and disabilities of slow learners. In general, the methods proposed were similar in the different schools. All stressed the imperative need for interest and motivation, for careful organization and presentation of appropriate steps in learning, for repetition and revision and for the immediate reinforcement of successful learning. The use of concrete modes of presentation and the value of a multi-sensory learning situation were stressed in many different ways. Individual and social aspects of learning were advocated and related to individual, group and class learning situations. The quality of these sections of the curricular documents was excellent and backed by creative, intelligent and informal discussion in the schools. Teachers in schools without a written curriculum, and those teachers in schools where a curriculum was not considered essential to education, discussed this aspect of their work at a similarly high standard. Some schools without a curriculum produced · guide-sheets on method intended to assist teachers to interact in pupil-determined activities in ways which fostered learning and sought to make it more effective for the pupil. There is no doubt about it: after the question 'What shall we teach?', the question 'How shall we teach it?' ranks high in the priorities of the project schools and is even posed in schools which might regard the first question as inappropriate!

Equally excellent and impressive was the attention given to the more fundamental aspects of teaching method. Use of the blackboard, presentation of charts and teaching aids, use of audio-visual hardware, and suggestions for classroom organization, discipline and class control featured in the more comprehensive and carefully prepared curricular documents. Some of these provided splendid support for teachers, and especially less experienced teachers, a fact fully confirmed by discussion with teachers fortunate enough to receive the support. Yet once more the fact must go on record: excellence of this kind was more closely allied to special schools and separate departments for slow learners in ordinary schools than to other forms of organization.

In their discussions of method teachers of slow learners frequently referred to their aims in the education of their pupils. It appeared that consideration of aims influenced decisions on method or were used to justify or explain decisions which had been taken. The most interesting examples of this concerned the basic methodological question of formal or informal learning and teaching, particularly as the aim–method relationship produced different answers. The aims stressed were usually personal–social, concerning self-realization, or self-expression, and self-control or self-regulation; and the place of these attributes in assisting pupils to take their place in adult society. Those teachers stressing control or regulation adopted formal methods while those stressing realization or expression tended to support informal approaches. The polarization was distinct, with the added interest that it arose from a common aim: that of preparing the pupil for adult society. There was, of course, a more balanced view – that both the above experiences are important for the pupil and contribute to his personal and social education through his exercise of discipline and freedom. In many 'middle way' schools the balance appeared to be associated with curricular areas, more formalized teaching in basic subjects being balanced by child-centred approaches in other subjects. Unfortunately, this balance sometimes reflected the importance attached to the subjects rather than the result of the analysis indicated above. In the less organized schools and in those where the concept of curriculum was not considered important, pupils often appeared to experience all the above approaches in the classes of different teachers as they moved through the school. This could be confusing for those slow learners who do not understand their teachers' beliefs and could regard such alternating experiences as further evidence of the unpredictability of adults.

The above discussion of the teachers' attempts to relate aims and method requires further comment. First, no absolute value can be ascribed to the different approaches, for quality varied in all. Secondly, in all approaches some teachers imposed their procedures on pupils without explanation or discussion, while others attempted to give pupils some insight into their purpose. Thirdly, very few teachers considered their own approach to aims and methods in terms of its effect on pupil *behaviours*, though this was possibly a result of the neglect of curriculum *objectives* in the schools. Fourthly, whatever the outcome, the fact that some teachers were acting in a manner consistent with their considered aims, attempting to work out values through practical classroom decisions, deserves note.

One negative feature of the curricular documents and discussion was the general failure to identify the relationship between methods and value outcomes of education afforded high priority by the teachers. To some extent this also reflects the lack of concern for objectives in the curriculum. Truthfulness, honesty, personal integrity, compassion, concern for others, co-operation, open-mindedness and objectivity are all qualities valued by teachers which form the expressive objectives in the curriculum. It is doubtful if such qualities can be taught directly. The contribution of curriculum content appears limited to biographical material from history, literature or religious education; and perhaps the most potent sources for such objectives are in the total complex of relationships affecting the pupil in the school. It is just such a complex of the total strategies of learning in the school which links up curricular objectives with teaching methods. In practical terms this requires the recognition that, in some situations, *how* a pupil is taught and learns may contribute more to certain curricular objectives than *what* he is taught or learns. This link between method and objectives was rarely discussed.

RECORDING IN THE CURRICULUM

In examining the forms of recording in the curricula from schools, and in discussing recording with teachers, the objective was to assess how far what was written down indicated what the pupil had achieved, and how efficiently the information could be related to the curriculum followed by the teacher. Most of the records submitted to the project were school records. They set out in detail just what the individual pupil had achieved in his passage through the school, usually at the end of each school year. In the basic subject areas they recorded attainment levels, standard test results or subjective assessments by teachers. In other curricular areas subjective assessments predominated, frequently accompanied by the results of school-designed examinations and indication of class positions. In most records there was assessment of personal and social qualities with some indication of persistence or effort, often separated for the different subjects. A summary brought together the information in a short personal sketch and indicated the degree and kind of effort required of the pupil in the future. Apart from the last point, it was exceptionally difficult to relate these records to the curriculum which the pupil had followed or the kind of teaching he had received, and they failed to provide a basis for assessment of either the appropriateness of the curriculum or the pupil's success in achieving the aims or the objectives proposed for him. In this form the records were a useful account of the pupil's progress through the school and, collectively, could be used to provide statistical information for purposes of inter-school comparisons or assessment against local norms; but they contributed little to curricular assessment.

The above records were supplemented in some schools by records of diagnostic testing in the basic subjects, usually in reading. Tests and sub-tests were identified, together with dates of testing and name of tester. In the better examples the tester's record script was included for examination, procedures suggested by the test were indicated and there was some comment at each testing on the pupils' response to the teaching proposed as a result of previous tests. These types of records were restricted to a narrow but important section of the curriculum. They were also infrequent in use, confined to approximately one in six of the schools. About the same proportion of teachers kept detailed records of their pupils' reading, showing titles of books read, with progress through them noted and dated. This type of record is useful, especially to teachers who take over classes, or receive pupils into their classes, as well as to headteachers or others who must supervise the work of class teachers, assess pupils' progress or arrange additional or special teaching for slow learners. But there were important omissions. Objectives for pupils were rarely projected at the beginning of teaching sessions (terms, etc.); clear indications of methods and approaches used were infrequent; progress was more likely to be shown by page numbers than by record of words successfully incorporated in reading vocabulary; language experience, class-work and vocabulary were not usually recorded for linking with reading; and the time the pupil had spent in the learning situation was rarely indicated. These omissions made it exceptionally difficult to relate the records back to the curriculum and learning experiences to which the pupil had been exposed and it was, therefore, equally difficult to assess the quality of either the teaching he had received or the curriculum followed.

In arithmetic/mathematics records were mainly confined to indications of the content of the curriculum covered by the pupil, an assessment of his competence in calculation or the use of processes with, maybe, an indication of topics given general coverage – for example, interest, rates, graphs. In primary schools following 'modern maths' curricula there might be an indication of concepts achieved with some brief note of standard, or of practical situations which the pupil had encountered. In extent and quality these records were inferior to those for reading.

Speech and language were accorded importance in almost every curriculum submitted to the project and this was reinforced continually in the comments of teachers in the project schools. But this importance was not reflected in the written records from the schools. Speech was noted – mainly in relation to difficulties; language was assessed globally (for example, good, average, poor, or on some qualitative scale A–E, etc.); differences in understanding or expression might be noted, again in general terms; and there might be an indication of personality in connexion with communication (for example, withdrawn, unforthcoming, uncommunicative, talkative, etc.). In some special schools, or where pupils were involved with remedial teachers or speech therapists, the records showed use of the *Illinois Test of Psycholinguistic Ability* and/or the Reynell test, with teaching programmes frequently designed to follow the theoretical pattern of the sub-tests. Records from these programmes were usually detailed and compared with successive test results. In one area visited an experimental programme had been devised, apparently out of the interest of the local educational psychologist, to meet the needs of socially deprived pupils entering the infant schools. The programme was based upon simple everyday situations within the experience of the pupils and appropriate sentence forms had been prepared for each. The pupils were drilled in the sentence form whenever the opportunity presented itself during their normally free play activities. Gradually the sentence forms were elaborated and related to slightly differing situations. In principle, the approach was similar to that of language programmes such as the *Peabody Language Development Kit*[16] and the *Distar* language programme,[17] in that there was massive repetition of sentence form with immediate reinforcement and subsequent attempts to generalize learning. The schools visited, however, did not use 'kits' or programmed material, relying on situations within the pupils' experience and recall, and on skilful reinforcement by the teachers. Records followed the sequence of the programme and teachers were aware of the structures and levels which were established by individual pupils. Judged subjectively on visits nine months apart, the success of this programme and the accuracy of records was remarkable, deserving more detailed assessment than was possible in the project.

The general level of recording in the language curriculum was less than adequate. There are some acceptable reasons for this: language is a complex activity which ranges over the whole curriculum; standard tests for classroom use are non-existent; most teachers are unaware of linguistic analysis which would assist their observation of language behaviour; and understanding of relationship between language and thought, and language and regulation of behaviour, is only just beginning to penetrate into the schools. It is doubtful if there exists an adequate system for recording pupil progress across the wide area of language behaviour.

Perhaps more damaging to language-deprived slow learners was the general absence of any serious attempt to record basic situations planned to develop language in a way which might assist subsequent teachers in their attempts to further the language skills of the pupils. An exception to this was one outstanding special school. Here, the development of audio-visual programmed teaching had led to definitions of experience situations outside school, to analysis of appropriate language content, to the briefing of teachers to feed in language in the out-of-school situation, and to the picking-up and reinforcing of the language in the subsequent audio-visual programme in the school. The definition and structure of the situation identified and reinforced the language content, and the link which emerged between situation, language and recording made a significant contribution to effective learning and its development.

Outside the basic subjects, recording was confined to indicating the content covered in the teaching offered to the pupils. Though the form of the records differed, this was equally true of both subject-based curricula and curricula based on broad subject fields, projects or centres of interest. There were few examples of any attempts to analyse situations in terms of concepts, processes or skills, to identify the levels at which pupils were intended to operate, or to show any circular or spiral progression through which concepts might have been extended or developed. In most records, the indications of the content covered were too general to allow any subsequent teacher to attempt the above analyses or to relate content to pupil achievement in knowledge, understanding or skill.

In short, therefore, it appears that there is reasonably efficient recording of attainments in basic subjects in those schools which keep records, that these records centre on reading and that they may be supported by diagnostic information. Though the latter information is not usually closely related to proposed teaching programmes, it is useful to other teachers who follow on with the pupil. Work in arithmetic/mathematics is less satisfactory, as is the recording of language curriculum and development. Outside basic subjects, records, where they exist, are general statements of content covered; they are without analysis, too general to support subsequent analysis, and therefore unsuitable for assessment of the curriculum or pupil progress.

Though the above account accurately reflects the general situation in the project schools, special note is required of the situation in some assessment and reception classes in special schools and in a number of primary-school classes involved with socially deprived infant pupils –

those discussed in the section on methods. In these recording was exceptionally detailed. Motor development, perceptual–motor links, perceptual development, speech and language, personal and social development, and general and specific learning difficulties were recorded in carefully thought out systems. Development was frequently broken down into small steps and pupil progress through the steps indicated with commendable accuracy. It did not always follow, however, that detailed recording was related to a specific programme or curriculum, for in some schools the records were regarded only as charting the development of the pupil. Another interesting feature of these curricula was where the recording system had sometimes been organized *first*, to be followed by a curriculum designed to *fit the records*. One result of this was that excellent records were not fully utilized in assessment of the teaching and/or curriculum in the class or unit, with consequent absence of attempts to evaluate procedures or identify the specific aspects of curriculum contributing to the progress of the pupils, a feature accorded importance by Wedell[18] in his discussion of this type of curricula.

EVALUATION IN THE CURRICULUM

This discussion is about measurement, assessment and evaluation in the curriculum of the schools. Measurement involves the use of a standardized test, as in word-recognition tests, or the count of identifiable elements as in a reading-vocabulary word count. Where such techniques are not possible, or not available, then teachers use structured assessments, usually on a three- or five-point scale, and these may be supplemented by non-standardized tests composed in the school. In between these methods are those which rely on tests which are not standardized in the full sense and indicate the 'level' or 'class' of the pupil's performances rather than a standardized 'score' which may be compared to a norm for pupils of the same age. Outside these methods are what might be termed general or impressionistic assessments which derive from a teacher's experience of the pupil and are completely subjective. All these methods of measurement or assessment were represented in the project schools, most schools using a combination of the techniques, though in a minority of schools any attempt at measurement or assessment was rejected as contrary to the educational beliefs of the teachers.

Evaluation is a concept wider than measurement or assessment but which includes them both. It is a process concerned with changes in pupil behaviour, particularly those influenced by the curriculum he has followed; so that in evaluation it is first necessary to establish if any change has taken place in the pupil's behaviour and, if so, the direction of the change and its magnitude. Measurement and assessment will produce the necessary information, albeit with different degrees of precision and reliability. It is at this point that evaluation takes over, for the change in behaviour must be set against all that is known of the pupil and the teaching he has received before a decision can be reached about whether or not the change is satisfactory and acceptable. Put another way, evaluation is a process in which the *anticipated* outcomes of the curriculum (the objectives) are compared with the *actual* outcomes of the curriculum (pupil behaviour).

In the project schools measurement made only a limited contribution, being confined to reading, number and spelling, and leaving relatively untouched the higher-order skills in these, as evidenced by the predominance of word recognition over comprehension in the reading-test records. Structured assessment was used more widely, in curricular areas outside basic subjects, in social competence and in personality development. Still wider was the use of general or impressionistic assessment. Less in evidence were assessments based on the techniques indicating levels of performance.

Special comment is required on the general or impressionistic techniques which were widely used in the schools. The subjective nature of such assessments has been mentioned above, but a further weakness of the method is the tendency, in generalizing about pupils, to overlook the many specific facets which make up the total behaviour of individuals. The technique is also more effective in indicating the kind of person the pupil *is* rather than what he *knows* or can *do*. In spite of these limitations, many such assessments attained a remarkable accuracy which seemed to rest exclusively on the sensitivity, insight and experience of the teachers making the assessments.

Another point of interest is that teachers, in documents and in discussion, rarely made the distinctions between measurement, assessment and evaluation which have been made above. Some of the criticisms of tests and measurements made by teachers (and by inspectors and education officers) appeared to arise from this lack of clarity. The criticisms, when analysed, were often criticisms of the limitations of the tests or measures as techniques of evaluation, a function which they are not designed to, and cannot, perform. Such a confused attitude cannot exist where the limitations of tests or measures are clearly understood along with their importance and usefulness in providing objective data which may be used in, and possibly enhance, the separate process of evaluation. Unfortunately this basic misunderstanding led, in some instances, to the rejection of tests or measurement and to a reliance on impressionistic assessments, the limitations of which have already been outlined.

Whatever the combination of measurement or assessment techniques, evaluation limited to evaluation of pupil progress was frequently recorded as satisfactory or unsatisfactory without being related to the curriculum. Where evaluation became the subject of inquiry, following a negative outcome, it was almost always related to an examination of curriculum content or teaching methods – both noted as strong features of curriculum in the schools. Conversely (and understandably), the outcome of evaluation of pupil progress was rarely related to curriculum objectives which, as the discussion has shown, were not usually defined with precision in the curricula of the project schools. The limitation of school records was another factor in the limitation of evaluation. There are two important points to be noted here. First, precision in the definition of curriculum objectives facilitates the design of records which are appropriate to the objectives; secondly, these records include the detail necessary for the achieved behaviours of the pupils to be related to the anticipated objectives defined in the curriculum. It was the absence of precision and detail in these two functions which limited feedback from evaluation in the project schools and consequently denied to them a valuable technique of curriculum refinement and development.

The above summary presents a general assessment of the situation in the project schools, but a question may be raised about the extent to which it reflects the situation in different types of schools. It has been suggested that the shape and precision of the curricula have been more notable in the segregated situations of special schools and classes and in separate departments for slow learners in secondary schools than in the less distinct situation provided by setting, banding or mixed-ability teaching. Recording also follows a similar pattern. As a result, the feedback from evaluation in the curriculum is more common and more effective in the segregated situation. Nevertheless, even there the main weaknesses noted remain as limiting factors.

The ultimate test of the curriculum is the response of the pupil to the situations and demands which face him as a young adult in the post-school world. In the project schools there were attempts to follow up pupils after they left school and to use the information in evaluation. This was most common in schools which had developed distinct school-leavers' programmes and kept detailed records of the pupils' activities and competencies in that part of the curriculum. Such courses (under various titles) were operating in half the secondary schools and two-thirds of the special schools. The special-school courses were the most detailed, followed by those in separate slow-learners' departments of secondary schools, and this may have accounted for both the superiority of recording and attempts at evaluation in these situations. Here, too, evaluation was more closely related to levels of pupil attainment on leaving school than to the curriculum the pupil had followed, so that assessment of post-school success (or lack of it) was related to the pupil's reading age, social competence level, etc., when he left the school. It was difficult to avoid the conclusion that this weakness was due to the failure to define precise curriculum objectives relevant to post-school tasks and situations and to record the degree to which they had been achieved by the pupil on leaving school.

FEEDBACK IN THE CURRICULUM

The term 'feedback' is used here to define the process whereby consideration of one aspect of the curriculum, its development or its outcome, influences attitudes, thought or action in relation to other aspects of the curriculum. In other words, feedback should generate interaction between different aspects of curriculum and between the curriculum and its objectives. There are three aspects of feedback to be considered: that which relates different sections *within* the curriculum; that which relates objectives achieved by pupils to anticipated objectives; and that which informs the learner about his progress towards anticipated curricular objectives.

Feedback and interaction within the curriculum are influenced by the shape of the curriculum itself. The discussion above indicated that curricula in project schools were strong on aims, content and method but weak on definition of objectives, recording of pupil progress towards objectives and in evaluation of the extent to which anticipated objectives had been achieved by the pupils. Most feedback occurred between the strong areas of curricula. There was a high degree of interaction between aims and methods fully brought out in discussions with teachers. In most schools the consideration of curricular aims powerfully influenced, if it did not determine, questions about free versus directed learning, about the degree of interaction between slow learners and normal pupils, about the nature of school discipline, about the extent to which pupil interest should determine method, about the desirability or otherwise of mixed-ability classes, and about topic, centre of interest or subject organization. Conversely, the success or otherwise of specific methods appeared to be a factor influencing aims, particularly in the emphasis given to self-expression, to self-regulation, to personal, social or academic aims, and to the relative emphasis on the individual or on the group. The selection of curriculum content was also influenced by consideration of aims and methods. For example, where there was a predominance of social aims, content was preferred which stressed social interaction and allowed curriculum organization based on co-operative projects. Where integration of knowledge was stressed, selected content often allowed for some team-teaching over broad subject fields. Concern with communication as an aim resulted in carefully structured content presented in separate areas of the basic subjects of language, reading and writing. The emphasis on pupil interest and motivation frequently exercised an important influence on curriculum content, particularly in those schools which accorded low priority to organized curricula.

To a great extent the lack of attention to detail in the written curricula and in discussion resulted from the weakness of curricula in defining curricular objectives. The weakness has been discussed earlier; here it is sufficient to reiterate that objectives form a practical link between curricular aims and classroom practice; they take account of the difficulties exhibited by slow learners and they contribute to increased precision in the selection of content and method. They also make it easier to relate outcomes of teaching and learning to the aims which should shape and guide the process.

The other weak areas of curricula were those of recording and evaluation. This was inevitable given the weakness in the definition of curricular objectives. As a result evaluation was only capable of identifying strong or weak areas of curricula and lacked the detailed information required to identify the precise content or method influencing the objectives achieved by the pupils. It has to be said also that the documentary weaknesses were not offset in discussions in the schools, for the kind of precision implied above did not appear to have high priority in the teachers' thinking. Moreover, though teachers made much of important curricular objectives difficult to define in observable behavioural terms, such objectives were only related to basic broad learning situations, and were defined usually in the press of discussion rather than in documents about curricula. The failure to identify the critical situations which dispose pupils towards important expressive objectives made it exceptionally difficult to assess or evaluate the effectiveness of much experience-based curricula.

There are some exceptions to this general situation. In the basic subjects, in practical subject areas (crafts, home economics, etc.) and in the curricula concerned with early motor–visual–perceptual learning, detailed definition of content implied objectives to an extent which allowed interaction between aims, content, method and objectives at a level of precision unusual in other areas of curricula. Similarly, evaluation in these areas directed attention to specific areas of curricula where revision or strengthening was required, though this aspect was less frequently exploited, the emphasis often resting on the degree of pupil progress, and feedback relating to the totality of the curricula rather than to its detailed parts.

In the curricular documents and in discussion with teachers, the concern with the progress made by pupils was unmistakable and consistent. This concern was reflected in the attention given to recording individual progress, especially in special schools, special classes and separate departments for slow learners in secondary schools. Most of the records seen were adequate while the best represented considerable thought by the teachers and development based upon experience. At first this might be taken to represent a concern to compare anticipated curricular objectives with the achieved behaviours established by pupils in the process of teaching and learning, but close analysis revealed that this was not so. The concern with pupil progress was real and commendable, but it was almost exlusively concerned with progress as such, and progress, generally or globally defined as 'getting better', appeared to become a general objective taking on something of the nature of an aim. Such progress was diligently sought after by teachers, usually without attempts to specify the final behaviour which would mark out the progress or the stages on the way to such fulfilment. Information from measurement and assessment of the general levels of achievement by pupils leaving schools was often related to the school curriculum, but the general nature of the information, together with the absence of specified, anticipated objectives with which it could be compared for evaluation, greatly reduced the effectiveness of the process in refining curricula. The benefits of the process were mainly in relation to skill and knowledge content and to methods, represented by closing gaps in the content, and the regulation of teacher control and pupil responsibility in the methods. But it was noticeable in discussion that the concern for achievement of more specific objectives was not a major priority in the schools.

The absence of clearly conceived or defined curricular objectives made detailed comparison of anticipated and achieved curricular objectives almost impossible in the project schools. Only in basic subjects, particularly in reading (word recognition), was there any real attempt to relate the pupil's performance to the teacher's expectations for him. Even in this the process was usually to compare the pupil's test score with norms for his age rather than to project a performance level to which he could aspire. In some schools retrospective use was made of the pupil's achievement by making him aware of his progress, in the process challenging the pupil to maintain it to the next test. In using this technique the third type of feedback appears, for the pupil is made aware of the level of his performance, there is reinforcement of his efforts and there is a challenge which may have a positive influence on his level of aspiration. Special schools, special classes and separate departments in secondary schools made most effective use of this approach with slow learners.

Outside the basic subjects any comparison of anticipated and achieved objectives was at a very general level, usually involving the impressionistic assessment noted earlier. In the absence of specified objectives, the impressionistic approach was inevitable but it was skilfully used by many teachers to influence sensitivities, attitudes and values in their pupils. The process demands intimacy between teacher and pupil if it is to be effective and its success also depends on sensitive counselling by the teacher. Fortunately this was an excellent feature of most of the work seen in project schools, with enormous influence upon the pupils in terms of the *kind* of people they are, or are becoming, and no praise is too great for what these good schools are achieving. It is unfortunate that the general attitudes to, and shape of, curricula in the schools restricts the opportunities for the more effective use of teacher competence in terms of the pupil's cognitive growth and his development of skills.

In some special schools the quality of teacher–pupil relationships implied in the previous paragraph was the sole motivator of learning for the pupils. There was no mistaking the skill with which the rapport was used to foster every aspect of the pupil's learning and motivation by making him immediately aware of his improved achievement. Though almost totally subjective and operating within the frame of reference of the special school, both pupil and teacher understood the process. There are two criticisms to be made. In some instances the pupil was unaware of, and the teacher appeared to have lost contact with, the reality which exists outside of special schools; the teachers gave absolute values to what were, essentially, relative judgements. There is always this danger, especially in boarding schools for slow learners, where there is not the discipline of the daily return to the 'real' world. One advantage of special classes or departments for slow learners in ordinary schools is that the teachers are more easily kept aware of the competencies of normal pupils and are thus less exposed to this danger. In the best of the project special schools outward-looking aspects of curricula were specially intended as a safeguard. The other criticism is of the tendency to prolong the 'pleasing the teacher' level of motivation. The quality of relationship referred to above creates this danger through the use of teacher-centred motivation at age and maturity levels where the pupil could become involved in more intrinsic motivation. Some very good special-school senior classes and secondary departments showed this weakness.

References

1. D. K. WHEELER, *Curriculum Process*. Hodder & Stoughton Educational, Dunton Green, 1967.
2. E. W. EISNER, 'Instructional and expressive educational objectives: their formulation and use in the curriculum', in W. J. Popham (ed.), *Instructional Objectives*, AREA Monograph 3. Rand McNally, Chicago, 1969.
3. P. H. HIRST, 'The logic of the curriculum', *Journal of Curriculum Studies*, **1**, 1969, 142–58.
4. N. C. KEPHART, *The Slow Learner in the Classroom*. Merrill, Columbus, Ohio, 2nd edn, 1971.
5. M. FROSTIG and D. HORNE, *Handbook to the Frostig Programme for the Development of Visual Perception*. Follett, Chicago, 1967.
6. A. E. TANSLEY, *Reading and Remedial Reading*. Routledge & Kegan Paul, 1967.
7. W. K. BRENNAN, J. M. JACKSON and J. REEVE, *'Look' Visual Perceptual Materials Handbook*. Macmillan Education, 1972.
8. S. A. KIRK, J. J. MCCARTHY and W. D. KIRK, *Illinois Test of Psycholinguistic Ability*. University of Illinois Press, Urbana, Illinois, 1968. (Distributed in UK by NFER Publishing, Windsor.)
9. J. REYNELL, *Infant and Young Children's Language Scales*. NFER Publishing, Windsor, 1969.
10. H. GUNZBERG, *Progress Assessment Charts*. National Association for Mental Health, 1966.
11. E. A. DOLL, *The Vineland Social Maturity Scale*. NFER Publishing, Windsor, 1947.
12. E. A. LUNZER, *The Manchester Scales of Social Adaptation*. NFER Publishing, Windsor, 1966.
13. D. H. STOTT, *Bristol Social Adjustment Guides*. Hodder & Stoughton Educational, Dunton Green, 1956.
14. P. R. MORRIS and H. T. A. WHITING, *Motor Impairment and Compensatory Education*. Bell, 1971.
15. W. K. BRENNAN, *Reading for Slow Learners: a Curriculum Guide*. Schools Council Curriculum Bulletin 7. Evans/Methuen Educational, 1978.

16. L. DUNN, J. O. SMITH and K. HORTON, *Peabody Language Development Kit*. American Guidance Services, Minnesota, 1968. (Distributed in UK by Educational Evaluation Enterprises, Bristol, and NFER Publishing, Windsor.)
17. SIEGFRIED ENGELMANN and JEAN OSBORN, *Distar Language*. Science Research Associates, Henley-on-Thames, 1969.
18. K. WEDELL, *Learning and Perceptuo-motor Disabilities in Children*. John Wiley, New York, 1973.

VI. The quality of the curriculum in the schools

Introduction

This chapter is about the quality of curricula in the project schools, which means that it presents a series of value judgements. It is important that the nature of these judgements should be clearly understood. The assessments and evaluations which are made are to be regarded as general and tentative, not as statements of specific and absolute values. This is consistent with the stated intentions of the project to 'map' curricular activities, to indicate relative merit in different curricular areas and to provide pointers which might assist in the selection and design of subsequent curriculum development projects.

The evaluations which follow are subjective; but they were generated from within the project team, and were not made within the schools evaluated. Observation in project schools, discussion with the teachers and assessments of their pupils – all by members of the project team or others experienced in teaching slow learners in similar schools – were combined with information from curricular documents and school records to form the basis for the evaluations. Two sets of circumstances added to the difficulty of evaluation: first, the restricted use of standardized tests or measures or even criterion-based assessments in the records kept by the schools; and secondly, the absence of clearly defined objectives for pupils in the curricula of the schools. It is not easy to judge whether or not a curriculum is appropriate or effective if the teachers responsible for it have not forecast the outcomes they expect or recorded the progress of pupils through the curriculum. Yet that was frequently the task which faced the project team in the schools.

One further point must be clearly established. The evaluations which follow are evaluations of the appropriateness and quality of curricula offered to slow learners in the project schools. They must not be generalized to the quality or standards of teaching in the schools, for the project does not offer any assessment of these, which were not part of the project brief. Similarly, the assessment of curricula is confined to the curricula offered to slow learners and must not be generalized to the overall curricula in the mainstream of the ordinary schools.

A framework for assessment

To assist with problems of assessment, in particular those of comparability between schools or between assessors, a framework was devised with two sections: basic subjects and general curricula.

BASIC SUBJECTS

Language, reading, spelling and number were the main concern, regarded as basic subjects, the core of communication skills and the vehicle for education. It was held essential that good curricula should achieve the best possible results with slow learners in these areas. Qualities looked for in language were: pupils' ability to express their needs, feelings and intentions in speech and to understand these when expressed in language by other persons; their willingness to express themselves to strangers; and the use of language appropriate to the situation. In reading, accuracy, comprehension and speed were looked for, together with interest in books, some selectivity and evidence of reading outside school. Legibility of handwriting and accuracy of spelling were checked, as well as ability to compose simple prose. Grasp of the number system and four rules, with the ability to apply them to money, linear measure, weight and capacity, were the touchstones for arithmetic, with some indication that skills were used outside school. Concepts of time and distance together with the ability to estimate outcomes of processes were also checked. All these expectations were, of course, relative to the age, level of intellectual development and personal maturity of the pupils. Interaction in the above areas was considered important; standards expected of pupils were assessed for appropriateness; checking, reinforcement and recording were noted. Consistency between aims, objectives, content and method was looked for, as was evidence of reviewing and revision of curricula.

GENERAL CURRICULA

In basic subjects there was some consistency between the curricula of schools within the groupings of primary, secondary and special schools, but general curricula were marked by wide variations both between and within the groups. During the first round of visits to schools it had become clear that curriculum variety could be handled only by assessing each school within its own frame of reference. In order to do this four main questions were applied in making assessments: 'Is the curriculum real?'; 'Is it relevant?'; 'Is it realistic?'; 'Is it rational?'

Though these questions make no assumptions about the detailed content of the curricula, it should be noted that education is regarded as a process in which it is possible to work for predetermined objectives, and to be selective about those objectives and about the content and methods which will assist the pupil towards them. The assumption is that the curriculum is an account of the result of selection in the school for which it is intended. Not all teachers in project schools accepted this view, some being critical and others rejecting it totally as anti-educational; and similar attitudes were expressed by some teachers at meetings and conferences. However, most teachers appeared to accept the assumption as fair and reasonable.

Some further explanation of the four main questions is required. In asking if the curriculum is real, we were looking for a relationship between the curriculum as school activity and the real world of people and things and happenings outside the school. The question on relevance asks if the above relationship is connected with the world in which the pupil lives, the world which *he* perceives and to which *he* gives meaning. The slow learner's perceived, meaningful and relevant world, though the essential starting-point for the teacher, is narrower than the real world and part of the task of education is to extend the slow learner's relevant world to include more and more of the real world; so both concepts are important. While the real and the relevant are concerned with both objectives and content, the issue of whether or not the curriculum is realistic is almost wholly concerned with objectives, behavioural and expressive. A realistic curriculum specifies objectives which, though relevant for the pupil, are also attainable by him given effort on his part which is reasonable for his stage of personal and intellectual development. This is important. To be unrealistic and over-demanding puts the pupil in a negative situation; to be unrealistic and under-demanding denies the pupil the joy and excitement of learning accomplished through recognized effort, an essential part of positive life experience for the child. Another point about the realistic curriculum is whether or not the teaching required is within the skill and competence of those who must teach the pupils. Finally, there is the question of the rationality of the curriculum. Rationality is about ends and means in curricula; about priorities which are the basis for selection of these ends rather than those, this objective rather than that, these methods in preference to others. Rationality requires some inner consistency between different sections and aspects of the curriculum as well as a recognizable relationship between the curriculum and the immature slow learner, his contemporary situation and the anticipated demands which will be made on him in adult life. The rational curriculum assumes that the process of education can be shaped through intellectual analysis and planning in a way which will ensure outcomes more appropriate and efficient than would be achieved by a 'mindless' process. One test of rationality is the extent to which curricular activities and their purpose can be explained to pupils without recourse to the exercise of authority or appeal to tradition. Where this is done successfully in a manner compatible with the pupil's stage of development, it not only extends the pupil's understanding of the educational process but involves him in it, with a positive effect on his motivation. This attitude to curricular activities was specially looked for and is different from what was commonly called 'child-centred' education in the schools.

This then is the framework which directed observation of the general curriculum and provided a basis for assessment. No special merit is claimed for it, though it was found to be useful by the project team, and it may well be that curricula which are real, relevant, realistic and rational have some chance of also being appropriate and successful, especially if basic subjects and communication skills are well established.

Evaluation of the project schools

Taking the above criteria, project schools regarded as successful were those which appeared to be achieving the minimum demands indicated for basic subjects and developing general curricula which satisfied the four questions when considered in relation to the pupils in the schools. The criteria do have limitations. They are school based, for project resources did not allow any follow-up of pupils who had left school, though data in the schools (where they existed) were taken into account. Table 4 sets out the data.

Table 4 Project schools assessed as providing successful curricula

	Primary	Secondary	Special	Total
All project schools	196	183	123	502
Project schools assessed successful	90	90	75	255
Successful schools as % of project schools	45·91	49·18	60·97	50·79

So far as *extent* of success within the project schools is concerned, successful schools made up approximately four in ten of the primary schools, five in ten of the secondary schools and six in ten of the special schools. It would not be unreasonable to project this level of success as representing a basic minimum likely to be found in the overall system of education. In doing so, however, there are reservations to be noted. First, the success is for work with slow-learning pupils; secondly, the success relates to meeting the needs of slow learners through appropriate curriculum; and thirdly, there are primary and secondary schools which successfully meet the needs of the majority of pupils making normal school progress, though not necessarily with their slow-learning pupils. The latter point is important and makes illegitimate any extension of the figures for successful schools beyond consideration of slow learners. It is of interest, though, that most successful curricular work with slow learners was being conducted in schools which were notable for their all-round competence across the range of their pupils.

Though the figures for secondary and special schools are far from satisfactory, it is, perhaps, the relatively poor showing of the primary schools which is the most disturbing feature. The relative failure of primary schools in meeting the needs of slow learners is a factor contributing to the problem in secondary schools. And it is a failure difficult to explain with confidence, though project experience provides some tentative suggestions. It is doubtful if the typical large, mixed-ability class found in most primary schools is the ideal situation for the teacher who must provide the individual attention, guidance and carefully designed learning situations required if the slow-learning pupil is to make optimum progress. And while withdrawal for teaching in special groups is arranged in some schools, the present ethos of primary education does little to encourage such arrangements. It is true that some teachers prove the exception to the above generalization, but they are the outstanding teachers and not typical of the general level of competence in primary classrooms. Further, because most primary schools are relatively small schools, attempts to meet the needs of slow learners through special classes in the project schools were not marked by success. In the typical situation observed (and in contrast with some of the data on special classes) the special class was a single class serving the greater part of the age-range of the school and frequently the repository of most of the children with behaviour problems in the school. Such classes were consistently remarked upon as dull, depressing, uninspiring and dismal situations for the slow learners in them. It should be said that this was in marked contrast with those situations in which a number of special classes offered slow learners some tangible progression as they followed their special curriculum. Primary schools are also handicapped by the pattern of development in many slow learners. The dullest of their pupils only begin to come to terms with basic literacy skills half-way through their primary-school years. Even if they are taught and learn appropriately, they will require special attention all through the primary school. Though such pupils enter secondary schools still retarded, they are poised for a breakthrough to literacy which can be exploited in good secondary schools.

The implication here is that the curriculum (and indeed teaching) for slow learners tends to be more successful in situations where there is a degree of separation which ensures that the problem presented by slow learners is recognized, defined and followed through – hence the contribution of departments for slow learners in a minority of primary and many secondary schools. For, as in the primary schools, those secondary schools with slow learners in mixed-ability groups were rarely meeting the needs of slow learners in a manner considered satisfactory by the project team. Like their primary-school counterparts, the average secondary teachers in these situations are so overwhelmed by the problems presented by the wide range in their groups that the needs of slow learners become a low priority, the individual slow learners becoming lost in the group. And the group in the secondary school may be with several different teachers and in different classrooms during the school day, another disadvantage for those slow learners who need continuous and consistent support if they are to learn successfully. The converse of this is that the successful departments for slow learners in primary and secondary schools achieve their success because they create, within the ordinary school, learning situations for slow learners which have much in common with those found in successful special schools. These situations were invariably marked by a high proportion of class teaching providing prolonged pupil–teacher contact with continuity of curriculum and teaching methods.

Quality in the curriculum

The process of education is a constantly changing process affected by international and national economic pressures, pressures within the educational system and pressures within the schools themselves, not least of which are changes in teaching staff which affect the distribution of teaching competence over the different areas of the curriculum. In addition there are changes in the materials and techniques available, often influenced by swings of fashion difficult to justify rationally. The population of pupils also changes over a period of time. In general competence, social and family background, pre-school experience, attitudes to education and teachers, motivation for learning, and even in their attitude to different curricular subjects and activities, pupils change in ways which have a direct effect upon the organization of curricula in their schools. As a result of all this, any description of a school gives a static effect to something that is in a state of constant though not necessarily perceptible change. A curricular weakness may well be a fading strength or an emerging competence, and only intimate knowledge of a school over a period of time will determine which. The project team did not have such knowledge, which is a strength of a good local inspectorate,

Table 5 Successful work with slow learners in curricular areas (rounded percentages and rank order for 255 schools rated successful)

Primary N = 90	%	Secondary N = 90	%	Special N = 75	%
English	46	School-leavers'		School-leavers'	
Environmental		courses	43	courses	52
studies	39	English	31	English	40
Mathematics	26	Parenthood courses	27	Perceptual training	28
Music	13	Environmental		Home economics	27
Perceptual training	13	studies	25	Art	19
Art	8	Social service	22	Craft	17
Physical education/		Integrated studies	21	Social service	17
movement	7	Craft	18	Parenthood courses	16
French	3	Home economics	17	Physical education/	
Craft	3	Art	17	movement	15
Drama	2	Mathematics	16	Environmental	
Science	2	Science	16	studies	13
Social service	1	Humanities	12	Mathematics	12
History	1	Social studies	11	Science	11
Humanities	0	Drama	10	Music	8
Religious education/		Music	9	Rural science	3
moral education	0	Physical education/		Integrated studies	1
Rural science	0	movement	9	Religious education/	
Social studies	0	Rural science	7	moral education	1
Geography	0	Geography	7	Social studies	1
		Religious education/		Drama	1
		moral education	4	Geography	0
		French	0	History	0
		History	0	Humanities	0

and this limits the value of their judgements. For the present purpose this preamble is a necessary introduction to a section which makes comparisons, however tentative, between different areas of curriculum and formulates generalizations based on the comparisons.

The 255 project schools rated as successful (see Table 4) were reviewed in terms of the relative effectiveness of different areas of curricula, and Table 5 indicates the percentage of work rated as successful in different curricular areas, arranged in rank order for primary, secondary and special schools. Percentages in the table are calculated for each group. There was some discussion about whether or not the successful schools should be shown as a percentage of schools offering the subject to slow learners. Scrutiny of the table shows that for many subjects this would have meant calculating percentages on very small numbers! As they stand, the figures give a true reflection of the extent of successful work in the curricular areas in a sample of successful schools. It has also been argued that few schools would offer, say, humanities, and geography and history, etc. This is a valid point. If, therefore, humanities and associated subjects (history, geography, social studies, religious and moral education) are taken together, successful work would be as follows: primary, 1 per cent; secondary, 23 per cent; and special schools, 2 per cent.

ENGLISH

The first observation on the data shown in Table 5 must be about the position of English. In the context of slow learners and the framework of evaluation detailed earlier, English is basic, consisting of everyday communication in speech, reading skills and the ability to put together a number of consecutive sentences in simple prose about some straightforward, everyday topic. Even allowing for the fact that the backgrounds of most slow learners put them at a special disadvantage with language, that they enter schools unable to cope with the language of early learning situations, that language may not have, for them, the interest and fascination it has for their brighter peers – the fact that only about half of the schools are successful in the basic English curriculum must be regarded as unsatisfactory. That language and reading are intimately related is a factor, and accounts for much failure in reading curricula, including the neglect of higher-order reading skills in slow learners, which is discussed in detail in the other publication from the project, *Reading for Slow Learners: a Curriculum Guide*.[1] There are language and reading difficulties created by the disadvantages of the pupils, but it is part of the task of the English curriculum to take account of, and compensate for, such difficulties. It appears that this is happening in only about half the schools and that, consequently, the very communication upon which education relies is not efficiently established for many slow learners, even at the restricted level indicated by their disadvantages and stage of personal development. Suggestions for language and communication curricula are discussed later.

HUMANITIES

The next cause for concern is the position of the humanities. The term is used loosely in the context of slow-learning pupils as meaning any study which contributes to self-realization; to concepts of what it means to be human and to communicate and interact with other humans; to becoming aware of the values which men have created to regulate relationships between individuals or between groups; and to appreciation of diverse human cultures and the forms in which they are expressed. This sounds complicated and cerebral when subjected to intellectual analysis, but there is a powerful affective side of the humanities curriculum which is about feeling for and with others, the acceptance of human differences, and even about reverence for life, which is intimately connected with the expressive objectives discussed earlier, and the contribution which teaching methods and total school relationships can make to the achievement of those objectives. These considerations lead to concepts, difficult to express in language, yet involving experiences which cannot come to full fruition until expressed and assimilated in language that allows for their examination and evaluation. But language is difficult for slow learners and less than adequately handled in half of their schools! It is hardly surprising, therefore, to find successful humanities curricula absent in primary and special schools, where there is a high degree of immaturity among slow learners, and present in only 12 per cent of secondary schools. However, the values of the humanities can be communicated under other curricular labels: how do these emerge from Table 5? The data are brought together in Table 6.

The data in Table 6 do not suggest that the objectives of humanities are widely covered in associated subject areas. Indeed, the data on social service and social studies suggest that, though there may be some incidental contribution to humanities objectives in social service, the failure to use the experience as the basis for social study, analysis and learning may severely limit the transfer potential of the experience. This is the point made by Lawton[2] and noted in Chapter III. It may be that slow learners in primary schools are too immature for this aspect of curricula, but this is not so in special schools where the discrepancy between social service and social studies is greatest and involves adolescent

Table 6 Successful curricula in humanities and associated curricular areas (percentages in 255 schools rated as successful)

Subject	Primary	Secondary	Special
Social service	1	22	17
Social studies	0	11	1
Religious education/ moral education	0	4	1
History	1	0	0
Geography	0	7	0
Humanities	0	12	0

pupils. The situation is more balanced for slow learners in secondary schools, though only one school in five has a successful social-service curriculum and no more than about one in ten back this up with a successful social-studies curriculum.

Religious and moral education

By any standard the position of religious and moral education must be rated disappointing. There is extensive literature on religious education which relates the curriculum and teaching to child development[3] and also on the moral development of children with reference to implications for education,[4] but there is little evidence from the project that it has yet influenced the curriculum in the schools. A similar comment has been made about the more concrete and specific materials from the Schools Council's development projects in the humanities and in religious and moral education.[5] So far as slow learners are concerned there is little indication of any contribution to humanities objectives from religious and moral education.

History and geography

The position of history and geography is equally disturbing. Little of quality emerged for history and the same could be said for geography apart from the 7 per cent of successful work in secondary schools. Yet work in both these subjects can be developed appropriately from an early age, and contribute to concepts of continuity and development in human societies and affairs, to concepts of co-operation between nations, and to understanding of the essential continuity between man and his environment which explains many cultural and social differences and contributes to the rational acceptance of them. Some contact with these ideas seems essential if the pupil is to relate appropriately to his natural and social environment, and it is difficult to envisage how any slow learner can be considered suitably educated without some awareness of these matters. Yet the absence of successful curricula in history and geography reduces the possibility of such awareness and limits the contribution of both to the overlapping objectives of the humanities curriculum.

Other curricular areas contributing to humanities

The data in Table 5 do offer some compensation. About two primary schools in every five are producing successful curricula in environmental studies which may contribute something to the humanities objectives. The same can be said for one in four secondary schools and one in eight special schools. About half of the secondary schools and special schools have successful school-leavers' courses which, though late in the curriculum, do offer some discussion and guidance relevant to humanities objectives. In secondary schools successful integrated studies (one in five schools) and home economics (one in six schools) also contribute to the objectives proposed for humanities; though integrated studies rate low in special schools, which show more success in home economics. Successful parenthood courses (one in four secondary schools and one in six special schools) also have a humanities content through consideration of the interaction in families and human relationships. Though this appeared true of a minority of the very best courses, the objectives of most were too frequently directed to the physical aspects of child care. Useful though these other curricular areas are, they cannot compensate for the low level of successful humanities curricula indicated in the data in Table 5, and this appears also to be the situation disclosed in the report, *Teaching Materials for Disadvantaged Children* by Gulliford and Widlake.[6]

ART AND CRAFT

The myth that slow learners are all 'good with their hands' has, quite rightly, faded from the schools in recent years, but it is still disappointing to find no more than one in five schools rated successful with slow learners in these areas. It is of interest, though, that the percentages of successful curricula differ little between secondary and special schools. Special-school teachers frequently point to their schools' lack of facilities and specialist teachers as limiting factors in these curricular areas, yet the limitations do not appear to have significant influence on the extent of successful work in special schools. Observation in the schools suggests that, although the special schools are inferior in facilities and specialist teaching, the curricula in art and craft are more appropriate to slow learners and more closely integrated with classroom work in other areas of the curriculum. A similar comment would be true of music also, with the added rider that the percentage of successful curricula is even lower than for the other arts in secondary and special schools. Primary schools do better, with music ranked fourth, though with only 13 per cent successful schools. Drama rates about the same as music in secondary schools but successful curricula fall to 1 per cent in special schools, rising only to 2 per cent in primary schools. This is very disappointing, as the growth of reciprocity to which drama contributes is an essential factor in bringing pupils to the stage in development where they begin to relate well to others and acquire the ability to see situations from another person's viewpoint. Both these competencies are essential for the achievement of objectives in the humanities and in moral education,[7] and contribute usefully to role-playing, a developing technique in both curricular areas.

PERCEPTUAL TRAINING

The attempts to develop perceptual-training curricula in primary and special schools are welcome, as they represent recognition in the schools of sources of learning disabilities unrecognized until recently. As the work must be considered experimental at present, attempts are perhaps more important than absolute success. The activities observed appear more effective as techniques which may prevent the development of disabilities rather than as remedial techniques for perceptual disabilities which interfere with learning. To some extent the work is too isolated from the rest of the curriculum. There need to be closer links between the perceptual training programmes and gross and fine motor activity linked with physical education and movement curricula, though it should be noted that the latter curricula also offer room for improvement (see Table 5). Perceptual training should also be linked with other curricular areas. Art and craft involve central perceptual processes, looking at and observing differences and similarities in shape, colour, texture, etc., which offer opportunities for the application of perceptual skills which, if exploited, might lead to more art and craft time being allocated to observation of these qualities in the environment. Literature, and especially drama, which involves the assumption of roles and reaction to others, is connected with the perception of persons and social interaction, skills which can be trained and should be trained more positively as contributing also to social competence and humanities objectives.[8]

MATHEMATICS

In this basic subject, with curricula mainly confined to essential skills and concepts, Table 5 indicates that successful curricula were observed in only one in four primary, one in six secondary and one in eight special schools. Because of the importance of this basic subject, curricular documents and reports of practice were re-scrutinized at a one-day conference by the project team and an authority on mathematics with slow learners and member of the project's consultative committee, Alec Williams. The following assessments and evaluations were formulated from the conference.

Primary schools

1   The primary-school curricula demonstrated a general lack of recognition of developmental factors relating to mathematics:

    a   The concept of readiness for learning was not well developed and there were few attempts to work out the implication of the concept for mathematics teaching.

    b   In the few documents which did attempt to do this there was no reference to the recent research which has questioned the quality and permanence of concepts generated by highly structured and readiness programmes. Consequently, the idea that pupil maturation should be carefully and sensitively followed in order to select the optimum time to introduce specially structured experience did not appear in any curricula. For similar reasons, there was no indication of awareness that some pupils might not be able to benefit from the readiness programmes which were proposed.

    c   At later stages of curricula it was too often assumed that all pupils of a given age would be able to complete successfully the learning tasks prescribed for a particular stage.

2   There was insufficient attention to the hierarchies of concepts and skills in the learning of mathematics:

    a   Few documents acknowledged that for most pupils concepts of time and weight come late in the sequence of concept development, and practice in schools was variable in this respect also.

    b   There was insufficient recognition that differences in the variety and quality of life experience could result in pupils demonstrating individual differences in both rate and patterns of learning.

c Many documents consisted of lists of topics to be covered, or processes to be learned and practised, presented in year levels with little connexion between the work of successive years or attempts to deal with similar topics or concepts in a maturational sequence of increasing intellectual complexity.

3 A great deal of attention had been paid to the presentation of work in many schools and this was often very attractive. However, some attractively presented assignments showed evidence of insufficient attention to the grading of work according to logical progression so that pupils could grapple with and master one difficulty at a time. There appears to have been some falling away of this important teacher skill.

4 Most documents placed much more emphasis on cardinal number than on ordinal number and the relationship between these aspects of number was not well handled.

5 In so far as curricula for slow learners could be isolated – not always easy in primary schools – there was an impression that such curricula tended to neglect the more practical, concrete, experimental approach to basic concepts which is the hallmark of modern mathematics teaching. This is unfortunate as, properly handled, the techniques should be easily adaptable to the concrete learning modes of most slow learners, though there are reports that some learning situations in modern mathematics result in slow learners 'going through the motions' without appearing to establish any permanent insight or learning.

6 A feature of the documents was the lack of reference to the child failing, whether in the general curriculum of the school or the curriculum for slow learners:

   a No attempts were made to indicate points of failure which would require reference of a pupil for closer assessment.
   b Few documents attempted to set out any additional guidance for teachers faced with failing pupils.

There seemed to be an unjustified and uncritical assumption that all pupils would make satisfactory progress.

7 The overall, general impression is that in primary-school curricula for slow learners there is urgent need to:

a Generate much better sequenced curricula which take account of the facts of child development and the known hierarchies in the emergence of mathematical concepts and skills.

b Institute assessment procedures which will regulate the pupil's entry into new learning situations.

c Develop recording systems that will foster practical learning situations which can be handled by teachers and pupils in normal school circumstances.

d Make some attempt to define the learning objectives in mathematics, with the terminal objectives realistically related to the pupil's potential and the intermediate objectives consistent with the points made in **a** above.

Secondary schools

1 Compared with primary schools, two points stand out in the secondary curricula:

a There are more frequent attempts to construct a special curriculum for slow learners.

b There is a more marked attempt to present curricula in terms of pupil objectives consistent with the ideas of modern curriculum development.

2 As far as developmental factors are concerned, the comments made about primary schools are also valid for secondary schools.

3 The absence of careful assessment was noted and no doubt accounted for the general failure to develop prescriptive methods in the curricula examined. This was demonstrated in:

a The general assumption that all pupils would be ready to enter the curriculum at the prescribed point.

b The failure to recognize that the most immature pupils would still be at the stage of concrete operations in their thinking and a few, possibly, still at the intuitive stage.

c In mixed-ability situations, a failure to discuss problems in presenting initial learning situations to groups of pupils whose learning modes might cover the intuitive to formal levels in the development of thought.

4 In the documents, a variety of aims was proposed for similar groups of pupils, ranging from those schools which limited the curriculum strictly to 'survival mathematics' to those presenting a programme of modern mathematics which seemed to be aimed more at interesting the pupil than establishing either understanding or practical competence.

5 Among the variety of curricula there were few attempts to present mathematics in a way calculated to make the pupil aware of a need for concepts and processes which would serve to increase his motivation for learning.

6 There was a tendency towards great reliance on textbooks, programmed learning or teacher-produced assignment cards which created danger from:

   a The restriction of the concepts and processes attempted through efforts to keep assignments within the pupil's reading skill, thus reducing mathematical content.

   b The danger of pupils working assignments mechanically and superficially, completing them without establishing any permanent learning.

   c The reduction of pupil–teacher interaction with the loss of opportunity to shape the pupil's learning.

7 Slow learners need considerable reinforcement of learning if it is to have the quality of permanence. In general, insufficient attention was paid to this in curricula, especially to the need to present repetition in many guises as a means of sustaining motivation in the pupil.

8 Many documents examined showed an excess of mathematical terminology and also inconsistency in the use of terms. For slow learners specialized terms should be kept to the essential minimum, and those should be used with careful consistency throughout the curriculum.

9 Overall, the secondary documents, at their own level, showed the same inadequacies as those from primary schools. They defined aims slightly more clearly but showed the same need for development of assessment and recording, leading to progressive development of skills and concepts.

Special schools

1 The curricula from special schools showed considerably more insight into the developmental needs of children learning mathematics. It was thought that this might reflect the higher proportion of teachers with advanced training, which included child development.

2 Less marked, but still better than in the other schools, was the attempt of special schools to sequence concepts and skills consistently with known hierarchies in development.

3 The approach to work at the readiness level showed:

a Greater theoretical understanding of the concept than in the primary or secondary schools.

b A continuing weakness in translating theoretical insights into practical programmes for pupils. For instance, documents often had more in common with student essays than attempts to define learning outcomes for pupils, and practice frequently failed to reflect the sophistication of the curricular documents.

c The same uncritical use of the readiness concept noted in the section on primary schools (**1b**).

4 The social arithmetic or 'survival mathematics' sections later in the curriculum were more carefully worked out than in most secondary-school material, as well as being more realistically linked with wider curricula such as school-leavers' programmes. But there were few examples of attempts to take mathematical experience and learning beyond the survival level. Practice here was in line with the curricular documents.

5 Between the initial readiness programmes and the final survival curricula the quality of the work presented fell off sharply. It is clear that:

a Insufficient attention is given to the problems of grading work aimed at competence in the essential basic skills.

b The problems of motivating learning need to be more efficiently and creatively tackled.

c Practical activities are neglected as sources of concept development and motivation (see **5** in the section on primary schools).

d There is a need to seek more efficient links between the learning and practice required to establish mathematical skills and the practical application of the skills.

6 In general, the special-school sample showed a clearer grasp of developmental aspects of mathematical learning than other schools but there was a failure fully to extend and challenge pupils, which means that it is doubtful if pupils have adequate opportunity to experience the excitement of mathematical insight.

General comments

1 It is stressed that, though the curricular documents are uniformly weak on developmental aspects, many teachers are influenced by these concepts in their work, school observation indicating that actual work might be better than the documents suggest. Nevertheless, it is an important aspect which should be more clearly reflected in curriculum construction.

2 There is a great need to encourage the framing of curricula in terms of pupils' learning objectives so that recording, assessment and feedback may also develop in an attempt to make the curricula more responsive and efficient in meeting pupil needs.

3 Recording requires special attention. The best systems examined rely too exclusively on the pupil demonstrating the concept or using the the skill on a single occasion in a specific situation. There is a need to develop systems which will record stages in skill and concept growth and in their application.

4 There is a need for much greater continuity of learning, certainly between the stages of education and frequently between classes in the same school. Many gaps in pupil experience, knowledge or skill are the result of lack of continuity rather than ineffective or inefficient teaching. Good curriculum development could do much to reduce or eliminate this weakness.

5 Many mathematical concepts such as pattern, symmetry, proportion, etc., can also be approached through art and craft activities. Such an initial approach might be useful with slow learners, yet it was not developed in the curricula examined. Similarly, work in visual perception and aesthetic visual awareness gives access to many mathematical concepts, but there was little evidence of this approach.

The mathematics curriculum is marked more by isolated attempts to solve specific problems than by general, rational curriculum development. There is a need for curriculum development in mathematics for slow learners which would:

a Develop practical operational situations which allow closer analysis of needs than was possible during the project.

b From these situations generate a developmental framework defined as sequences in the growth of knowledge or skill described in terms of observable pupil behaviour.

c Begin to work out methods of recording progress which, in addition to describing what the pupil has achieved, give some indication of subsequent teaching approaches calculated to promote further achievements and understanding for the pupil.

d As a result of the above, not only offer guidance about which concepts and skills are essential, but also suggest approaches and define levels of learning necessary to meet the needs of the pupils.

There are a number of factors contributing to weakness of mathematical curricula and teaching which should be noted. The subject appears to have special difficulty for slow learners; the mathematical education of general teachers is not of a high standard; there have been radical changes in the approach to the subject in recent years; decimalization and partial metrication have created additional problems for teachers; inflation has changed values in a way not easy to assimilate and has made mathematical material and textbooks out of date. On the other hand, schools are slow in making use of simple electronic calculators which remove the drudgery of computation for slow learners, giving rapid results which can assist the pupil in understanding the usefulness of arithmetic and mathematics. Teachers take different views of this development, which will require careful consideration at the early readiness stage if it is to be efficient. Little was seen in project schools of Nuffield Primary Mathematics, the Midlands Mathematics Experiment, Mathematics for the Majority and its continuation materials, or of the SMILE (Secondary Mathematics Individualized Learning Experiment) materials,[9] at least so far as slow learners were concerned. The general view of teachers was that the materials and approaches have not yet been formulated in terms appropriate for the least able sector of the school population. The project team concur with this, and it appears also to be the view of Gulliford and Widlake.[10]

SCIENCE

Successful science curricula were operating in one in six secondary schools, one in nine special schools and one in fifty primary schools. Scientific method is about the identification and definition of a problem, the assembly of information relevant to it, orderly thinking about the relationship between knowledge and materials which might be relevant to the problem, the arrangement and manipulation of materials in a way calculated to throw light on the problem, observation of the outcome of the manipulation, and the relation of observed outcomes to the initial problem in order to reach a conclusion which can be tested. The process is concrete, rooted in perception, while sensory input imposes a discipline on cogitation. In the best curricula this concrete process was fully exploited in work with slow learners in the concrete operation stage of thinking; the science was linked with the observational, perceptive aspects of art and craft; and language was exploited with attention to precision and accurate description. Close integration of work in science with other areas of the curriculum was a consistent feature of good science teaching, most frequent in secondary schools and to a lesser extent in special schools. The same applied to primary-school science, though the occurrence of successful curricula for slow learners was rare even in schools which had established reasonable success with other pupils. It is difficult to account for this, though it may be that the large, mixed-ability primary class deprives the slow learner of the teacher intervention necessary if the pupil is to formulate his own conclusions.

Whether or not actual materials were in use, the influence of Nuffield Junior Science, Schools Council Nuffield Science 5–13 and Nuffield Secondary Science[11] was unmistakable in curricular documents and work observed in schools. This was true in the larger group of less successful curricula as well as in the successful examples. Indeed there was sometimes little to choose between these on paper. The difference was in the skilled teaching which converted anticipated objectives into actual objectives achieved by the pupils – a pertinent reminder that though good curricula anticipate learning, they do not guarantee it; for that, good teaching is also required.

The less successful curricula and teaching cannot be overlooked, for some contact with scientific method, together with an awareness of science as a process which has contributed splendidly to the state of man, must be considered essential in anyone who is to claim even basic education. Particularly important is an awareness of the *limitation* of this essential tool of man. It is also difficult to accept that anyone can be considered educated for the modern world without some awareness of the need for objectivity of thought and judgement to which science teaching should contribute. The unsuccessful curricula and teaching had little of this about it – science being regarded exclusively as a body of knowledge, facts to be communicated and remembered. This was often the result of the inadequate science education of the teachers, but some well-qualified science teachers had this attitude born of their too ready acceptance of the intellectual limitations of slow learners. Another limiting factor is that teachers attracted to work with slow learners appear to have arts rather than science backgrounds, and may therefore not fully understand the importance of scientific awareness and the contribution it may make to the education of their pupils.

Also absent from curricula for slow learners was any real attempt to develop a science of man, apart from some teaching in biology and one school using Bruner's curriculum for the study of man.[12] The social sciences, individual or social psychology, sociology, social anthropology, economics, economic geography, economic history, cross-cultural studies, etc., appeared to have little influence on curricula. Not that they would appear as formal subjects, but they might have been expected to have some influence on work developed in topics and to contribute to the pupil's awareness of the human situation and his place in it. These social sciences are the link between science and the humanities, and exploitation of the link is necessary if slow learners are to acquire any unified awareness of their social and natural environment which includes some idea of the variety and continuity of the human state

A further comment is required on science in the special schools. The successful work was mainly based upon the methods developed in modern primary-school science teaching which are appropriate for most pupils in the senior classes of special schools. Perception, observation and language were very well exploited, though in some instances took over to the disadvantage of science objectives. Otherwise, much of the content of science curricula took the form of useful knowledge. Knowing how to wire an electric plug, or change a tap washer, or even knowing that plants grow better if fed and watered, or that two parent animals are required to produce offspring, *is* essential knowledge which slow learners should possess. But such knowledge has nothing particularly scientific about it unless questions are asked which lead to investigation of the principles and laws which regulate these things. In most special schools the science curriculum failed to go beyond the level of fact or skill. This trend was also noted, though less frequently, in some secondary schools with separate departments for slow learners.

It appears that, though there are examples of good curricula and teaching in science, such examples are too infrequent to justify satisfaction about science in the education of slow learners. In this curricular area there are the beginnings of appropriate teaching materials and guidelines for teachers, though they need modification and development to meet fully the needs of slow learners. The main requirement is for courses to improve the scientific background of teachers of slow learners and to introduce them to scientific curricula and teaching, not only in the physical sciences and biology, but also in the social sciences, so that the contribution of the latter to the humanities is not overlooked in the curriculum.

SCHOOL-LEAVERS' COURSES

School-leavers' courses have been noted as a possible source of limited contribution to the humanities; here they are discussed in their own right. Table 5 indicates that over half the special schools and two in five secondary schools have some success with courses for school leavers, though the courses do not all use that title: 'RoSLA Course', 'Life Adjustment Course', 'Learning for Life' are examples of alternative titles in use. Many of the courses incorporate some element of social service which has been assessed separately, and in a number of schools work experience in factories, shops, offices, market gardens, parks, garages, etc., forms part of the course. Regulated introduction to work experience is the exception rather than the rule, but a few schools achieve this by placing pupils in Senior Training Centres, in Rehabilitation Units, or in the few experimental school-leavers' centres organized separately to serve an area or as part of the local education authority provision in further education. One special school had its own 'work-experience' annexe and another turned classrooms into workshops for a limited period for each group of leavers, using real work brought in from a Senior Training Centre, in a commendable effort to simulate workshop conditions. Increasing use is being made of 'linked courses' or 'taster courses' in colleges of further education as part of school-leavers' courses, and experience in the college workshops is regarded as part of work experience. Careers officers contribute to some but not all of the courses, their involvement being more frequent in the special schools. In secondary schools a similar comment applies to the involvement of careers teachers, though this is less frequent in schools with well-established, separate departments for slow learners. In such departments there is a tendency for committed heads of departments to be concerned with job placement, which might be legitimately regarded as the sphere of the careers officer, and this comment also applies to some heads of special schools and/or their careers teacher or teacher responsible for school-leavers' courses.

There are some very positive aspects of the work with school leavers. The courses look outside the school, to the world of work which the pupils are about to enter and they contribute to a healthy widening of curricula, an extension of relevance and an increase in motivation for learning. In many ways the courses provide opportunity for the transfer and application of established skills into situations wider than the school can provide yet still subject to some control and supervision by the teachers, for example, in moving about the environment, visits and work experience. The social interaction is also important. Pupils are required to interact with people less intimate than family and friends, who have less clearly defined roles than teachers and are unable to concentrate exclusively on the pupils, a distinction slow learners need to be aware of before they leave school. Within the school itself, the best courses achieve subtle changes in the relationship between teachers and pupils which make a distinct contribution to preparing the pupil for the world of work, and which are essential if outside experiences, and especially work experience, are to be reinforced by the counselling required by slow learners. Such counselling, of course, takes place as part of the pupil's experience in the linked courses, practical workshop time and in the work-experience centres. The intimacy of work and guidance here more than makes up for the remoteness from real work situations. For the most immature pupils the classroom workshop simulation noted above appears to provide a positive and necessary first step on the way to a wider working world, though the experience is not necessary for all slow learners.

There are also some common weaknesses in school-leavers' curricula:

1 Too much was claimed for them by many teachers. Pupil attitudes are difficult to change, and change, when it occurs, takes considerable time to establish. Some of the attitude changes expected from the courses were quite unrealistic and rarely attained by the pupils. In less efficient curricula there was a failure to provide counselling and guidance by teachers which amounted to a naive belief in the effectiveness of unstructured, unreinforced experience with slow learners. This was a feature of much work experience in open industrial situations. Many teachers appeared to have a simple faith in the amount of time which workers can devote to pupils on work experience, and the effectiveness of what workers can explain to slow-learning pupils. Both these beliefs may arise from lack of industrial experience in the teachers, and they are responsible for

inadequate or ineffective counselling offered to pupils following many work-experience programmes.

2 There is often a too ready assumption that work experience will teach social skills, and an associated failure to realize that this is a *transfer* situation of immense value for *established* social skills but with little to offer in their absence. Where this weakness was present in curricula or teaching, the general social competence curriculum which should prepare for work experience was usually absent or ineffective.

3 In some courses basic preparation was neglected. Pupils were observed, on link courses and in work experience, who had not been taught the basic technical vocabulary required before entering the new situation.

4 Follow-up of the experiences in school was poor in some courses, not only in terms of counselling, but also in terms of the use of the experiences to motivate work in the basic subjects or other areas of the curriculum.

5 As in most other areas of curricula, the actual behaviours expected of pupils were often inadequately defined.

6 Recording systems were often ineffective and incapable of providing the information required by teachers faced with the task of producing progressive assignments designed to add to the pupil's experience, skill or knowledge.

In the project secondary and special schools, the school-leavers' curricula ranked highest in terms of successful curricular work, though it was not rated successful in about half of the curricula examined. Though there is much activity in the schools centring round school-leavers' courses and work experience, few secondary schools follow up the post-school career of their school leavers. In special schools such follow-up is more frequent, but it is at a general level, concerned with the overall question of the number of pupils successfully holding jobs and avoiding social failure. Very rarely is the post-school information collected and analysed in a way which would allow teachers to use it as a source for development of school-leavers' courses or, even more important, the whole curriculum of the school. In another sense also, the school-leavers' curriculum operates in a vacuum. The curricular documents showed little evidence of awareness of research and the same was manifest in discussion with teachers. Together with the neglect of appropriate local follow-up of pupils, this lack of awareness led to a decision that some attempt should be made to assemble information about the employment

Table 7 Factors affecting work adjustment of slow learners (response to questionnaire of 119 careers officers in England and Wales)

	Careers officers' ratings					Total rating score	Overall rank
	5	4	3	2	1		
Personal inadequacies (ranked in section)							
1 Inability to concentrate and persevere	45	47	16	5	2	473	1
2 Lack of initiative in carrying out instructions	14	36	45	17	3	386	2
3 Inability to communicate (personal inadequacy)	17	41	26	25	5	382	3
4 Inability to establish relationship with fellow workers	13	25	38	34	4	351	5
5 Poor attitude to authority	7	22	28	41	16	305	14
6 Lack of discretion in attempting new tasks at work	5	16	26	47	18	279	18
7 Physically unfit for manual work	0	3	12	42	56	188	25
Deficiencies in acquired skills (ranked in section)							
1 Inability to understand instructions given orally	12	33	37	26	4	359	4
2 Inability to carry out simple mathematical calculations	15	26	35	25	13	347	6
3 Poor reading ability	12	30	27	31	13	336	7
4 Inability to follow written instructions	17	17	29	33	17	323	11
5 Inability to communicate orally (lack of vocabulary, poor syntax)	11	23	29	34	14	316	13
6 Inability to write legibly and accurately	6	21	30	37	19	297	16 =
7 Lack of aptitude in operating machines or handling tools	5	16	34	48	10	297	16 =
8 Poor spelling ability	4	11	16	40	42	234	20
9 Lack of general background knowledge inhibiting day-to-day conversation with others	5	9	19	32	48	230	21 =

	Careers officers' ratings					Total rating score	Overall rank
	5	4	3	2	1		
External factors influencing inadequate adjustment (ranked in section)							
1 Lack of job satisfaction	14	24	28	32	15	329	8
2 Poor attitude of employer to slow learners	7	25	36	39	7	328	9
3 Inadequate briefing on job requirements	5	28	38	32	10	325	10
4 Lack of parental interest	8	28	29	36	11	322	12
5 Poor attitude of workmates to slow learner	5	18	36	44	11	304	15
6 Rejection of vocational guidance by parents	5	11	30	37	30	263	19
7 Rejection of vocational guidance by pupil	3	5	21	49	34	230	21 =
8 Inadequate post-school follow-up	6	12	10	27	54	216	23
9 Lack of interest of careers teachers	3	7	6	35	59	190	24
10 Lack of interest of careers officers	1	3	5	34	67	167	26

experience of slow learners in the areas of the local education authorities which had nominated the project schools. The objectives were:

a To direct attention to important aspects of employment experience
b To do so in a way which schools might relate to their curricula
c To encourage schools to establish their own follow-up studies in a way which would assist development and reinforcement of curricula.

A questionnaire was designed based upon a review of literature,[13] and information derived from the project. It consisted of three sections: personal inadequacies, deficiency in acquired skills and external factors influencing inadequate adjustment. Within each section items were rated as: very frequent cause of poor adjustment in the work situation (5); fairly frequent cause of poor adjustment in the work situation (4); often a cause of poor adjustment in the work situation (3); occasionally a cause of poor adjustment in the work situation (2); and rarely a cause of poor adjustment in the work situation (1). The questionnaire was sent to the careers officer in the 135 nominating LEAs, and 119 were completed and returned. Table 7 shows the number of careers officers making each rating; and the items are ranked by total rating score, the ranks shown both within each section and overall.

In addition to the ratings presented in the table, careers officers commented on their experience with slow learners. Some of these comments which have relevance for the curriculum may be of interest to teachers, but first two points must be made about the questionnaire items. One careers officer writing in the project questionnaire about 'poor attitude to authority' suggested that this depended on who was exercising the authority. In an earlier study Wilson[14] had also made a pertinent point about the lack of understanding of the term 'authority'. The pupils in his survey, when asked what 'authority' meant, gave diverse answers. Another careers officer thought that the question on 'lack of aptitude' needed qualifying in that where routine work was concerned it was of small importance, but where anything approaching skill was concerned, appropriate aptitude was a major consideration. Further comments on pupils are now grouped under appropriate headings.

Timekeeping. Poor timekeeping was a major cause of difficulty. It was mentioned by several careers officers and was often coupled with absenteeism. Typical of the comments made were:

> 'Inability to get up and go to work'
> 'Lack of self-discipline because of home conditions leading to absences'
> 'Bad timekeeping'
> 'Inability to adjust to harsher industrial attitude towards timekeeping and attendance'.

Slowness. Many careers officers pointed out that slow learners were often too slow in the work situation. Their remarks are typified as follows:

> 'Slowness in performing task – thus out of gear with work team'
> 'Where teamwork is essential, a slow worker affects bonus rates'
> 'Slowness in comparison with other workers'
> 'Slowness in learning work skills'
> 'Poor adaptability – low transfer of skill from familiar to new tasks'
> 'Inability to adjust to the normal speed of production'
> 'Pace of work faster than at school'
> 'Learn routine tasks but fail to carry out at an acceptable speed'.

Perseverance. The slow learner's reluctance to face difficulties was commented on:

'Tendency to give up and leave in face of a difficult spell at work'
'Lack of staying power'
'Lack of persistence'
'Inability to establish a work pattern'
'Lack of work habits'
'Lack of concentration and sustained application'
'Unable to cope with a full working day'.

Lack of experience of simulated working conditions (this obviously contributes to many of the other difficulties):

'Lack of training in employment-type situations'
'Lack of realistic work-preparation schemes'
'Lack of understanding of expectations of other workers'
'Lack of properly equipped workshops, particularly in ESN schools, to prepare pupils for vocational training for factories'
'Unfortunately, many factory jobs are performed at high speeds and involve teamwork in production'
'Lack of confidence with fear of unknown'
'Lack of opportunity to sample work situations'
'Inadequate work experience and lack of knowledge of work routine'.

Personal relationships. Failure in personal relationships was seen as the major cause of poor adjustment to the work situation. Comments of careers officers included:

'Lack of sensitivity to others'
'Lack of ability to cope with leg-pulling'
'Inadequate briefing on employers' expectations of personal behaviour'
'Teachers encourage them to talk on equal terms and this continues on starting work; this sometimes upsets the foremen and charge hands'
'Lack of understanding on part of workmates'
'Inability to distinguish between instruction and criticism'
'Unwilling to make their deficiencies known for fear of ridicule'.

Training. Many careers officers spoke of inadequate training in industry and the inability of slow learners to take advantage of it when available. Under the heading of training, they made the following remarks:

'Inadequate supervison in early days by employers/supervisors resulting in mistakes which damage young persons' confidence in themselves'

'Inability to retain less simple job instruction/knowledge'

'Lack of co-ordination'

'Lack of ability to cope with more than one job or instruction at a time'.

Attitudes and values. Careers officers commented on the attitudes and values displayed by some pupils leaving school:

'Peer groups which value non-employment'

'Differing values about the necessity of working'

'Failure to maintain contact with employer – for example, not reporting illness'

'Influences of close friends'

'Tend to prefer to adopt a life-style that does not include work'

'Negative work ethic'

'Inability to see the point in going to work'.

Parents. Parents are criticized mainly for unrealistic aspirations:

'Parents are reluctant to recognize limitations and aim too high'

'In cases where children are from professional homes, parents are reluctant to admit of their [the children's] inadequacy for more demanding work. In many cases they [the parents] look for and often find jobs which are beyond a slow learner's capability. Overemphasis on social status of a job'.

Health and hygiene and first aid. Some typical comments were:

'Lack of knowledge of simple first aid and attention to personal health and safety'

'Dirtiness, smelliness and dirty habits'

'Poor personal hygiene'.

Lack of initiative. The comments indicated pupils being immature and having difficulty in anticipation and decision-making:

'Inability to anticipate next task if supervisor has neglected to tell him'

'Problems regarding public transport'

'Unwillingness to travel any distance'

'Lack of confidence'

'Inability to make decisions'.

Careers guidance. Careers officers made comments which indicate that some pupils do not receive adequate careers guidance or fail to make use of it where it is given:

'Failure to use the careers service'
'Task is outside the competence of the individual'
'Often unaware of own limitations'
'Unrealistic aspirations'
'Variation in school careers provision'.

Motivation and job satisfaction. This is perhaps the most difficult aspect for pupils unable to aspire to jobs at the level of skill which promotes interest:

'Lack of motivation'
'Lack of prospects'
'Boredom or lack of ability to find motivation in any work situation'
'Boredom'.

Teachers of slow learners might, with benefit, make their own analysis of Table 7 and the associated comments, relating them to curriculum and teaching in their schools, not merely in the school-leavers' course, but throughout the school. The school-leavers' course is concerned with the *transfer* of established knowledge, skills and attitudes into situations nearer to the world of work, or in assisting pupils to anticipate that transfer. Very little new learning can be expected except on the basis of established knowledge and skill. One analysis of Table 7 shows that, of the twenty-six items, eleven are the direct concern of curriculum and teaching in the school; six rest on aspects of the pupil's personality which might be affected by curriculum and teaching; only two are due to personality factors unlikely to be affected; and seven are external factors which the school could not be expected to influence. On this analysis, seventeen out of twenty-six items might be affected by appropriate and efficient school curricula in a way which would reduce the post-school difficulties for slow learners. It is difficult to be content with 'inability to understand instructions given orally', ranking fourth; 'inability to carry out simple mathematical calculations', sixth; 'poor reading ability', seventh; 'inability to follow written instructions', eleventh; and 'inability to communicate orally', thirteenth – all in the upper half of the factors creating difficulty for slow learners.

HOME ECONOMICS

Examination of the data of Table 5 indicates that home economics ranks fourth for successful work in special schools and eighth in secondary schools. Approximately one in four special and one in five secondary schools have success in meeting the needs of slow learners in the home economics curriculum.

The general curriculum of home economics has expanded considerably in recent years. It is no longer concerned only with cooking, needlecraft, housework, etc., nor with the exclusive fostering of wifely skills, and it is rapidly expanding as a subject for both sexes. For normal pupils it has come to embrace much of what might be termed household science, some economics, biology (especially in terms of reproduction and child care), some elementary psychology of human relationships, and many of the objectives noted above for humanities. It could be argued, of course, that the focal point of home economics is still the home. But the home is no longer seen as exclusively that of man and wife and family, for the knowledge, attitudes and skills learned in home economics are seen as equally applicable to the man or woman remaining unmarried, left alone as a single person or parent, or responsible for home-making for a group of people living together by choice or circumstances. Communication is seen as being of central importance and this generates concern for language in the home economics curriculum, while the precision required for some of the skills involves mathematics and measurement. Because people are affected by environments, among which the home is important, home economics is concerned with the aesthetics of colour, shape, texture and their combinations, and thus art and crafts enter the home economics curriculum.

The aims implied here are very broad indeed and lead to a variety of objectives. So broad and varied are the aims and objectives that home economics could become the central point of the school curriculum for slow learners, a situation closely approached in a few special schools. In secondary schools the separation of the home economics curriculum and teaching from other subjects is an effective barrier to such a focus but the aims and objectives remain consistent with it.

It was noted above that in some science curricula with slow learners the general subsidiary, educative objectives appeared to take over and detract from the science objectives. In work with slow learners home economics appears to be in a similar situation. The broad objectives are valid, pertinent and necessary for slow learners, and home economics should contribute to their achievement. But this must not be done at the expense of the basic life-support skills which are the core skills of the home economics curriculum. It is absolutely essential that slow learners leave school with at least well-established beginnings of the skills needed to feed, cleanse, clothe and house themselves satisfactorily; with some awareness of what is involved if this must be organized for a family group; and with some reasonably clear understanding of the processes, social and biological, which establish, control and maintain a family in our culture.

If these important basic objectives are to be achieved, then slow learners face extensive learning tasks. Success in the tasks will require from the teacher clear curriculum objectives, careful planning of well-graded learning experiences, subtle motivation of the pupils' learning, sensitive manipulation of levels of aspiration, adequate repetition and reinforcement of successful learning and the generalization of established skills to new and varied situations. The process makes intense and continuous demands on pupils and on the teacher; both need to concentrate on essential objectives. It would be wrong to assume from this that home economics must ignore the wider though subsidiary objectives. What is required is the realization that, while teaching for such objectives is not a priority task for the home economics teacher, the application of the relevant knowledge and skill from other curricular areas is offered wide scope within her subject. To make the most of the opportunity requires careful planning, the fostering, with insight, of interaction between curricula, and effective co-operation among teachers.

In attempting to meet the important, critical demands made on them by the needs of slow learners, home economics teachers are not assisted by the design of most schools. First, the departments are usually provided in splendid isolation; secondly, layout and equipment are as far removed from a home as a hospital ward and almost as clinical; thirdly, the model flat, when provided to offset the clinical effect, is itself artificial and rarely has a lived-in appearance; fourthly, the arrangements made in many LEAs for assembly or purchase of ingredients add to the artificial aspects of the curriculum. However effective present arrangements may be for those pupils who take the subject to the levels of public examinations, or aspire to teach it, or apply it in institutional management and similar careers, problems are created where the objective is to teach individual and family life-support skills, especially where the pupils are handicapped by learning difficulties. The differences between the home economics room and the home create problems of transfer for slow learners which reduce the relevance of the curriculum for many pupils, with an adverse effect on their motivation to learn.

Though the criticisms in the previous paragraph apply more directly to secondary schools, they also have validity in special schools. In purpose-built special schools the basic separation of the housecraft room is usually a feature of the design, and the room itself has the unfortunate features of the home economics rooms noted above. In some special schools, where LEA or headteacher misguidedly insists that only specialists can teach life- and family-support skills to slow learners and teaching is by visiting specialist teachers, the expensively provided housecraft room remains even more isolated, unused for part of the school week. That many special schools successfully overcome these disadvantages owes nothing to the design of the home economics rooms. Their success arises from the fact that they are small schools with the intimacy which that confers; that the school organization is based upon the class with a class teacher, which improves interaction between home economics and other subjects; that the home economics teacher can concentrate exclusively on curricula for, and teaching of, slow learners; that the reduced pressures on the home economics room allow additional teaching for pupils who need it; that teaching groups are about 50 per cent smaller than in secondary schools; that many home economics teachers in special schools also teach other subjects to classes in the school, again assisting integration; that, in some special schools, skilled teachers of slow learners, efficient housewives in their own right, and often assisted and supported by experienced home economics advisers, develop curricula and teaching in housecraft which is specially suited to slow learners.

Markedly absent from curricula in the schools were attempts to integrate craft teaching with home economics through the contribution of both to the home and the life-support skills noted above. If the inter-action of home economics and craft is to take place, and if the integrated studies are to become a focal point for the curriculum in which knowledge and skills from other areas of curricula are applied, then there is a need for substantial reconsideration of the manner in which home economics and craft facilities are provided in schools, particularly in special schools. The home economics areas in which skills are taught in a highly struc-tured manner might be smaller, even more specialized and provide for even more individualized teaching. The areas for the application of the skills might be less specialized, closer to home conditions and calculated to contribute to effective transfer of skills. There should be walls, windows, doors, etc., which can be knocked down, built up, painted, papered, etc. Sinks, drains, light circuits, water systems, central heating systems should be designed so that faults can be simulated, assessed and rectified. Slow learners may thus learn to do effectively things which are within the competence of the lay person and, more important, learn to judge effectively when the assistance of the expert is both advisable and required.

Subject time might be blocked so that the home economics routine could be more closely related to home and family routines and the curriculum content and materials used should be brought closer to the world which the pupils experience, though presenting it at its best. This means that objectives should be more consistent with a world in which the economic and social differentiation of sex roles is fading, routines of living are becoming both more streamlined and more democratic and the home is becoming the focal point for entertainment and the communication of information through radio and television. For slow learners, all this should affect the whole curriculum. Not only craft, housecraft, art, etc., focus on the home. Television or film presentation of material in other subject areas could be presented in the home economics centre and built into the routine in a way which might foster effective use of television as the slow learner's main link with his wider natural and social environment and with the arts. The extension of videotape facilities, including better programme material and video-recording facilities in LEAs and schools, should make this kind of approach more feasible in the future. Even if the approach is considered unnecessary or even undesirable for normal pupils, the size of contemporary secondary schools is such that the development of these facilities for slow learners and non-academic pupils would be a practical possibility. There is no indication of this type of integrated approach in the curriculum documents or project reports, and it is possible that the conditions criticized above inhibit its development. It may well be that an experimental development project is required which, from the drawing-board, combines the curricular and design concepts. Such a project implies co-operation between LEAs and the Department of Education and Science in a special- or secondary-school design experiment.

MUSIC*

In Table 5 the ranking of successful curricula places music fourth for primary schools (13 per cent successful), fifteenth for second schools

* The project was fortunate in having the advice of David Ward, Organizer of the Music with Slow Learners Project (1968–76) based at Dartington College of Arts, and Clare Cook, a teacher with wide experience and success in teaching music with slow learners, and advanced training and experience in teaching slow learners in ordinary and special schools. (Clare Cook's work in music with slow learners is featured in 'Music making', videotape 7 in the series *Teaching the*

(9 per cent successful), and thirteenth for special schools (8 per cent successful). It appears, therefore, that successful music curricula might operate in approximately one in eight primary, one in eleven secondary and one in twelve special schools. The following discussion is based upon a paper by Clare Cook, based on curricular documents, discussion with project workers and access to recordings made during the project.

Sound, with its qualities of pitch, tone and rhythm, surrounds the slow learner during his waking hours. This is an advantage in that sound is part of life experience; but the disadvantage is that familiarity often leads to reduced or restricted perception of sound. Most slow learners, therefore, need to learn to listen. For them, learning to listen must start at a very simple, primitive level, preferably when the pupil is young. However, the curricular documents suggest the need for much more extensive and careful attention to this aspect of music curricula for slow learners. Apart from this, much that is written about music for slow learners would apply equally well to all pupils.

In general the curricular documents and school visit reports suggest curriculum and teaching dominated by listening to music at later levels of tune and melody together with singing. In all situations, including in special schools, slow learners have difficulties in these aspects of the curriculum because the above early experience has been neglected. This relationship is not always recognized by the teachers.

In addition to concentration on early listening skills, most curricula for slow learners would be improved by increased emphasis upon and opportunity for music-making by the pupils. A start can be made with 'barred' or 'Orff' instruments played in a relaxed manner with a rhythm which relates to bodily movement, clapping, and chanted or speech patterns leading to simple melodic work. Good teaching brings fun and enjoyment to the work. It also links the work with the early experiences noted above as well as leading on to simple composition by the pupils.

Composition starts with experiment and looking for new sounds. Pupils acquire 'banks' of sounds, which they later organize into rhythmic patterns. There is a role here for creative teaching which assists the child to explore rhythm, tone, pitch, dynamics, etc., without reducing the unique personal feature of the work, and retaining fun and enjoyment. Very simple 'sign systems' which allow children both to write and read

Slow Learner, produced by the Inner London Education Authority Television Service (1975). The videotapes are on sale or for hire from Guild Sound and Vision, Woodston House, Oundle Road, Peterborough, PE2 9PZ.)

tunes prove helpful and prepare for later, more orthodox reading of musical notation. Group and individual work as appropriate add variety and allow the teacher to take account of different needs and abilities among the pupils.

General class teachers have expressed diffidence about their ability to handle activities such as those noted above. Yet there are sufficient examples of good teaching by such teachers to suggest that the diffidence of the many is not justifiable. However, the teachers need leadership from music advisers through practical courses followed by continued stimulation and support. Television series could be designed to assist and could be included in school activities. And teachers should be made more aware of the open-ended, experimental nature of the activities which create opportunities for pupils and teacher to learn together. Similar support is needed for aspects of the curriculum concerned with musical understanding and appreciation. Here it is important that slow learners should have opportunities to listen to a wide variety of 'live' music. Performers should visit the school and children should attend performances. Children should also have opportunities to perform for others, as giving as well as obtaining pleasure from music is an experience which holds many benefits for them.

Enjoyment, emotional expression and an alternative means of communication figure among the claims made for music in the curriculum documents. What needs to be clearly recognized is that the quality of these features of the music curriculum may well depend upon the quality of teaching and learning in the curricular activities noted above.

RELIGIOUS AND MORAL EDUCATION

Reference has already been made to the possible contribution of this area of the curriculum to humanities objectives, emphasizing the role of moral education, and indicating the relevance of child developmental concepts to religious education. Table 5 indicates the low percentages of successful curricula: 4 per cent in secondary schools, 1 per cent in special schools and nil in primary schools. In rank of successful curricula the subject is among the lowest in all three types of schools. The low status of this curricular area was the source of much heart-searching and doubt among the project team which manifested itself in long discussion in the project consultative committee, where many different and mutually opposing views were expressed. At the invitation of the project director, and with agreement of the committee, Ron Barnes, a member of the consultative committee, reviewed all the relevant curricular documents presented by the project schools. The section which follows is based upon his paper, and takes account of views expressed in the consultative committee and by teachers in the project schools.

The curricular documents indicate that teachers of slow learners exhibit the variety and degree of belief and the range of ethical attitudes which are to be found in any group of teachers. They show the same concern about the place of religion in society, its place in the life of the school and its specific place in the school curriculum. But teachers of slow learners also recognize the difficulties they face with their pupils: difficulties of language limitation, conceptual immaturity, lack of 'time perspective' and, in adolescence, a capacity for belief not matched by intellectual development.

Perhaps due to the difficulties of the subject for slow learners, the curricular documents are markedly traditional in approach. Insightful discussion of religious education for slow learners did not issue in new or experimental approaches to teaching, a situation substantiated by reports from school visits. In the ordinary schools corporate worship was directed at the 'normal' pupils, not necessarily wrong in the circumstances, but often making the experience meaningless for the slow learners. In mixed-ability situations similar comment could be made about the teaching. Separate classes for slow learners and special schools had curriculum content more closely related to slow learners though often simplified to a point where the 'story' or 'history' element almost excluded any religious content. Reports of special-school assemblies suggest a similar situation. In the best, however, the sense of participation and 'togetherness' allied to enjoyment appear to have benefits for the pupils irrespective of the religious content.

If the religious education curriculum is to be improved then certain general points deserve closer attention in the schools. For the slow learner religious teaching *must* remain close to his experience, it *must* be appropriate to his phase and level of development, and it *must* use language he can understand. Curriculum content must also reflect these features. Content might focus upon birth, growth and the life-cycle of the individual. The element of *care*, involving parents, extended family and neighbourhood, could be stressed, leading to the idea of *concern* of persons for each other. At an appropriate point death itself might be introduced as a natural part of the life-cycle. Care and concern can be related to the school and the pupil's experience in school. They may also extend to animals and plants as living things different from but closely related to people. In developing the work, skilful teaching can develop in the pupil a sense of awe and wonder. These experiences are not of themselves religious but, together with care and concern, form elements of religious experience. Only the individual teaching can relate these elements to the teaching of Jesus and the sense of God in a way which might have meaning in the life experience of the slow learner. Whether or not anything happens for the pupil in the way of religious experience or belief may depend upon other things such as family background and experience, or even some spiritual element which cannot be subjected to rational analysis. It is doubtful if any slow learners can be 'taught' to believe in God, or even if such an attempt should be made; but the religious education curriculum should at least create the possibility that religious experience might happen for some pupils.

The approach to the religious education curriculum with slow learners is subject to the comments on curriculum development and quality made in other parts of this report. And the possibility of spiritual elements should not be allowed to interfere with efforts to make the teaching and learning aspects more efficient. If these objectives are to be achieved in mixed-ability situations then there must be more careful consideration of the 'common curriculum' as well as improvement in preparing slow learners for their participation in it.

The religious education curriculum must also take account of people from different ethical and cultural backgrounds with religions other than Christian. These differences will exist in many schools and among their slow learners. Some attempt must be made to promote tolerance and respect for different religious beliefs. In this the teacher of slow learners faces the same task as colleagues who teach normal pupils. The task is made much more demanding because of the special difficulties experienced by slow learners in this area of the curriculum.

LANGUAGE AND COMMUNICATION

It is fitting that a chapter concerned with quality in the curriculum of the project schools should conclude with further consideration of the English language. Spoken English will remain for many slow learners the main vehicle of their education and the sole means of contact with their fellows and with their natural, social, cultural and political environments. For the most handicapped of these pupils, the spoken word, reinforced by the visual images of television and film, will be their sole means of contact with what is sometimes called the heritage of our literature. 'Poems and Pints', a television programme from workers' clubs, is a more likely source of contact with verse than the *Golden Treasury* or the *Oxford Book of English Verse*; imagery and imagination may gain from the folk-singer an immediacy which goes back beyond the age of print; Trollope,

Dickens, Galsworthy are more likely to be known through the television screen than through the school textbook. In all there is a primacy of the spoken word. For other slow learners, where the threshold of literacy has been crossed but where the desire to read is still latent, the experiences mentioned may be the impetus leading to books and literature. And for all slow learners this must be a common objective vigorously and efficiently pursued. Even for the least able members of the community, the ability to read at the level of their competence gives them a confidence and independence which is an important factor in their ability to relate to a literate society. *Reading for Slow Learners* spells out the primacy of language. The definition of reading stresses the necessary concepts and language to which the printed word must be related, and the need for a language programme to run ahead of, and to prepare the way for, the reading curriculum. The point is made that it is not *reading* which is comprehended, but *language*; that print turns spoken sentences into visual forms encompassing meaning in a way that requires release by the reading process if meaning is to operate and the language is to be understood. But the link between spoken language and reading is not one-way. Reading taught as suggested in *Reading for Slow Learners* reinforces language skills at the spoken level. At the comprehension levels, reading directs attention to deeper language structure; to the role of words in sentences; to the importance of word sequences; to sentence shape; and to explicit and implicit meanings.

Observation in project schools, perusal of curricular documents and discussions with teachers suggest the following observations on language teaching and activities in the project schools.

Language and the slow learners

1 Curricular documents and teachers emphasize that, compared with their normal peers, most slow learners are retarded in spoken language when they enter school and are likely to remain so throughout school life.

2 There is agreement that, except for those pupils with specific language disability amounting to a separate handicap, most slow learners speak and comprehend language when they enter school.

3 There is general agreement that the inadequate language of slow learners usually reflects:

   a Impoverished, general life experience

   b An inadequate language background in home and neighbourhood c Generally retarded intellectual function.

4 Though unable to explain why it should be, most teachers have experienced slow-learning pupils who are exceptions to the generalizations of **1** and **3** above:

  a Because language was superior to background experience

  b Because language did not reflect inadequate language experience

  c Because the language of the pupil appeared superior to his general intellectual level.

5 Almost all teachers can provide examples of pupils with poor backgrounds and inadequate language models who are, nevertheless, making normal progress in school.

6 While most slow learners show cognitive or experiential reasons for language inadequacy, some appear to be inhibited by factors of personality – not being very forthcoming, etc.

7 In some most seriously retarded pupils all three factors (experiential, cognitive, personality) combine to inhibit language functions.

8 Many slow learners show greater competence in the language situations of home and neighbourhood than in those of school.

9 It is commonly found that slow learners have not fully exploited the experiences which have been presented to them, usually because of inadequate perception of details, qualities or relationships in the situations.

10 Though general language competence is a reasonable indicator of the rate of progress which may be expected once initial reading skills are established, it is not such a reliable indicator of the degree of difficulty which pupils will experience in establishing basic reading skills.

Language curricula in project schools

1 Almost all curricular documents and teachers emphasized the importance of language curricula for slow learners.

2 Concurrent with, and independent of, the work of the Bullock Committee, teachers in project schools emphasized what the Bullock Report, *A Language for Life*,[15] defined as a language programme across the curriculum.

3 Most teachers and curricular documents stressed that:

a The language curriculum should relate to the pupil's experience and begin with the language possessed by the pupil

b The language curriculum should be concerned with the extension of the pupil's experience and its incorporation in extended and enriched language usage

c The quality of communication would regulate the slow learner's relationship to others in the post-school environment and might well be a critical factor in his success or lack of success.

4 Though about half the project schools of all kinds were judged to be achieving the objectives of **3a** and **b** with adequate competence, there were serious inadequacies among the remainder, many of which appeared as weaknesses in successful schools:

a Classroom-bound language teaching which failed to capitalize on existing pupil experiences and was unable to provide extended experience

b Failure to carry over and exploit in the classwork relevant pupil experience and even experience and situations generally organized by the school

c In practical situations, over-concern with enumeration and reference aspects of language creating static concern with nouns, adjectives and articles to the neglect of verbs, adverbs, prepositions and conjunctions reflecting action sequences, interchanges and relationships in situations observed and encompassed in language

d Neglect of perception as:

i A means of creating need for language

ii A process shaped and made precise by language

iii A means of identifying, classifying and relating qualities and events experienced in the environment

iv A means of becoming aware of self, and of relating inward feelings to externally perceived situations and relationships – a necessary process if there is to be reciprocity arising from feeling for and with others and understanding their uniqueness as well as one's own

e Over-concern with the expressive aspects of language to the neglect of receptive aspects, and associated failure to understand the importance of receptive language functions in the slow-learner's awareness of, and relation to, people and his environment

f Neglect of non-verbal aspects of communication in their relationship to speech and language:

   i Failure to exploit the relationship between situation and language

   ii Neglect of specific teaching on the need to observe eye contact, gesture, bodily attitude, etc., in conversation and communication

   iii Missed opportunities to train pupils in the use of visual cues for attention, pause, interlocution, etc., as a means of controlling and regulating verbal communication through techniques of perception

g Over-concern with striving to shift or alter language codes with pupils inefficient in the selection and use of registers within established codes

h The neglect of reading by the teacher as a means of widening the literary awareness of slow learners beyond their reading competence, and associated neglect of reproducers (tape players, tape/slide programmes) in exploiting reading

i Failure to exploit fully radio, television and film to stimulate discussion, increase awareness of literature and drama, and make current affairs more interesting in an effort to improve language usage

j Concern with reading and written communication at a level unsupported by the pupil's language development, with the danger that the former may inhibit the latter

k High proportion of teacher-directed questions in language interaction which:

   i Require only yes/no answers

   ii Are directed to named individuals, rather than to the group followed by designation of the pupil who is expected to answer

iii Represent failure, on the teacher's part, to distinguish between the legitimate questions designed to test memory and/or learning and the question designed to start conversation

l Reluctance of some teachers to give pupils a chance to talk

m Excellent child-care or parenthood courses neglecting the opportunity to assist the adolescents in acquiring knowledge and insight about situations and behaviours calculated to foster language development in young children (this appears equally true of secondary and special schools)

n In general, primary schools, secondary slow-learners' departments and special schools were aware of the need for general language stimulation, though the quality of presentation to pupils varied. Only a minority, however, showed equal awareness of the slow-learners' need for specific, structured learning in selected language areas. In mixed-ability secondary schools language teaching tended to be at a level appropriate to the 'normal' pupils. Modification and accommodation to meet the needs of slow learners were not good.

Language and school organization

1 Primary and special schools appeared to regard language as the concern of every teacher and every area of the curriculum. Similar attitudes existed in separate departments for slow learners in secondary schools. In mixed-ability classes in secondary schools, the need for this was recognized, but it appeared very difficult to achieve in practice at levels relevant to all the pupils.

2 In secondary schools with classes moving around among teachers and classrooms according to a timetable frequently organized on a subject basis, it is exceptionally difficult for such subject teachers to:

a Be familiar with the language levels of each group of pupils

b Alter their own language to suit successive classes at different levels.

3 Where mixed-ability classes move around, the task indicated in **2** above becomes a within-class task involving discrimination between individual pupils. This is so difficult as to be almost impossible for subject teachers, usually without special training in dealing with wide ranges of ability and often without insight into what is required both of them and by the pupils.

4 Where there is a separate department for slow learners in secondary schools there may be confusion about responsibility for language between the teachers of slow learners and teachers in the English department. Many curricular objectives may be left to the other by each, to the disadvantage of the pupils.

5 The appointment of language co-ordinators with responsibility for language across the curriculum recommended by the Bullock Report[16] may do something to regulate the weakness outlined in 4. However, in many schools the development will introduce a tripartite relationship between language co-ordinator, subject department heads and the head of department for slow learners. It would be foolish and unrealistic not to anticipate problems in relationships and communication from this development. They may not be dissimilar to those existing between heads of slow learners' departments, school careers masters and careers officers, or between the head of department for slow learners, school counsellor and school educational psychologist.

6 There was little doubt, however, that in many secondary schools there was failure to communicate about the language needs of slow learners across subject department divisions. In primary schools, too, continuity between classes was often less than desirable and was the source of many gaps in the language curriculum. Language co-ordinators could undoubtedly bring improvements in both these situations.

7 The other breakdown point, transfer from primary to secondary school, will require special attention if the situation of slow learners is to be improved. It requires:

a Improved means for recording and communicating language competencies

b Better contact between co-ordinators and teachers in primary and secondary schools

c Clearer definition of LEA language policy and of the roles of advisers for language and those concerned with slow learners

d A clear definition of the responsibilities of the respective head-teachers.

8 In some very good secondary schools, those approaching the concept of language across the curriculum fostered by excellent English departments, the standard of reading among slow learners was particularly disappointing. This appeared to result from a belief that interest in and excitement about English literature would be followed by improvement in reading skills. There are slow learners, even in excellent secondary schools, who need careful, efficient and continuous teaching in reading, supported by sound language experience and curriculum if they are to establish reading skills at a level which will guarantee permanence before they reach the end of statutory education. The needs of these slow learners must not be overlooked.

9 The weakness described in **8** was not noted in primary schools, special schools and those secondary schools maintaining well-organized departments for slow learners throughout the school. Circumstances predisposing to the weakness were:

a Mixed-ability organization in secondary schools, where the concept of special teaching or specialist teachers for slow learners had been rejected

b Mixed-ability organization in secondary schools where the prevailing philosophy dictated abandonment of withdrawal teaching in upper forms

c Lack of special provision for slow learners in secondary schools

d Provison for slow learners in secondary schools which was abanddoned in the final years in the interests of integration in general RoSLA activities for non-examination pupils.

The language curriculum in general

Statements of objectives for the language curriculum were absent in almost all the curricular documents from the schools in the precise form required to identify them in the behaviour of pupils. But it would be grossly unfair to criticize the teachers in the project schools on this account. The fact is that insufficient is known about the processes which support the acquisition of language or the sequences for development of language skills to allow any precise definition of behavioural objectives in the curriculum. The best to be hoped for is the definition of objectives in such general terms that they approximate to statements of aims and are of little value as aids either to the specification of pupil language behaviour or to description of situations which common experience suggests might foster efficient or extended language behaviour – that is, 'process' situations from which 'expressive objectives' in language usage may emerge. Indeed, the situation is not only inadequate: it is confused. Those to whom teachers might legitimately look for specific information on language and its development can offer only approximate generalizations or loosely defined models.[17] There is much to be done if a 'language for life' is to operate across the whole curriculum with clear objectives, and avoiding the danger of mistaking activity for achievement. The Bullock Committee which produced *A Language for Life* excluded from its work the majority of pupils who form the population of this study. Nevertheless, the aims indicated for pupils in general appear appropriate for slow learners and, if the argument in this study is correct, should contribute to the concept of a common curriculum. It is when language co-ordinators arrive at definitions of the pupil behaviours and competencies anticipated at various levels in the language curriculum that consideration of the different potentials of pupils will become important. Which objectives are to be common? Of these, which may be established at a common level? And for which will the levels of awareness or familiarity suffice for slow learners? Are there any objectives which may be ignored for slow learners? If so, why? Are they important? Or are there other more important objectives with prior claim on limited time? If so, what are they? And why are they considered more important? What are the common 'process' situations? Is there any discernible priority among these for slow learners? Is the balance of curricula between expressive and receptive objectives the same for all pupils? If not, why not? And how do the needs of slow learners influence priority and choice? How is adequate language performance to be measured or assessed for 'normal' pupils? In what way will progress and achievement be recorded? Will these systems adequately meet the needs of slow learners and their teachers? If not, how are they to be altered or modified? So the questions go on; appropriate answers will require the involvement of teachers with experience of slow learners throughout the development of the new approaches if their pupils are to share in the common curriculum without losing out in the consideration of their special needs.

Suggestions for curricular extension

Notwithstanding the confusion and uncertainty which exists in relation to the language curriculum for slow learners, certain tentative suggestions may have some value. There is a need to shift the consideration of language from the present almost exclusive concern with its external, reference function, and to include other aspects of language. Some general objectives might be considered which relate to the following aspects of the language curriculum:

1 Language as a regulator of the pupil's own behaviour:

   a Language used to restrict or control behaviour

   b Language used to generate appropriate behaviour

   c Language used to delay behaviour, to interrupt or divert behaviour

   d Language used to anticipate behaviour which may be required in an emerging situation.

These general objectives widen the context of language to perception of persons and situations, anticipation of future events, consideration of actions, effects and consequences. Development will be (generally) from the imposed, to the overt and the covert levels, the latter involving the internalization of language and its relation to thought processes.

2 Language used to influence the behaviour of others:

   a Choice of register appropriate to situation

   b Selection of tone, pitch and vocabulary appropriate to the chosen register

   c Regulation of gesture, bodily attitude, etc., to accord with **a** and **b**

   d Observation of the other person as the basis for selection of **a**, **b** and **c**

   e Engagement of the other person in the communication process, selection of appropriate approach, opening, etc.

   f Maintenance of interaction, eye contact, pause, non-verbal invitation to intervene, non-verbal expressions of agreement, question, request for repetition, encouragement, etc.

   g Balance of suggestion, request, command, etc., in the verbal interaction

   h Accurate perception and interpretation of verbal content and non-verbal signals from addressee

   i Use of **h** to modify continually addressor's language and non-verbal attitudes.

The above language skills involve the whole of social and moral development. They move from an exclusive concern with external circumstances to interpretations which rest in reciprocity, in the endowment of the other with the drives, constraints and moods of the self, as well as with the same planning competence as recognized in the self. The other person is finally recognized as a perceiver as is oneself, but a perceiver observing from a different viewpoint. Perception is now seen as a two-way process. The connexion of all this with cognitive, conative and affective development will involve the whole of the social and moral curriculum, humanities, arts, and indeed the wide awareness to which every aspect of the curriculum should contribute.

3 Language as an instrument of thought:

    a Language as an aid to enumeration, identification, correspondence and classification

    b Language used to identify relationships between classes, overlapping classes and cross-classifications

    c Language used to accompany and identify succeeding steps in solving a problem in concrete, external terms

    d Language used overtly to short-cut manipulation of a concrete problem situation

    e In concrete problem situations, the substitution of language for manipulation, with the manipulation of the situation used to test conclusions arrived at through the use of language

    f Verbalizing of a concrete problem and working it out in language which reflects the internal processes of assimilation and accommodation in reaching a solution

    g Gradual internalization of the language processes noted above

    h Acceptance of a problem in verbal terms and thinking through covertly to a verbal statement of a solution

These are steps in a process which reflects but also assists cognitive development, and which is applicable in almost every area of the curriculum and, therefore, legitimately involves all teachers.

4 Language as an expression of feeling and emotion:

    a Depends initially and continually on self-perception

b Is encouraged and fostered by readings from appropriate literature, including poetry and drama

c Is fostered by dramatic activity, role play, etc., which also contribute to the reciprocity required by **2** above

d Is frequently more easily handled in relation to other people

e Requires some of the skills of **1** above if the pupil's feelings are to be expressed in an appropriate, acceptable and controlled manner

f Represents an essential development of empathy and reciprocity if **2** above is to be a warm and concerned, rather than cold, process.

This area of language development is critical. It involves perception, thought, emotion, empathy, self-concept and reciprocity with others. It brings together the external and internal function of language, fosters the understanding of others based upon self-realization and is a main contributor to positive social interaction and co-operation between individuals. Slow learners can develop these skills, though initially they have difficulty with control aspects. If more serious thought is given to careful analysis, teaching and practice of the total communication process there could follow extensive improvement in this area of language curriculum.

5 Language as a vehicle for imagery and imagination:

a This use of language is rooted in accurate and rich perception of people, places and objects associated with the inner perception of feelings which may be reciprocally attributed to other persons

b In one sense **a** is required for a full appreciation of literature

c Imagery, defined as the ability to experience as present situations, persons or objects once subjects of sensory experience but no longer present, provides the material for imagination and is the half-way house to concepts. In imagination images may be placed in relationships impossible in the real world of the senses and the pupil may come close to the experience of the poet. In imagery, for instance, he can bring together all the different trees he has ever experienced, defeating time and space and moving to the 'tree-ness' that is the beginning of a concept.

d The sound element of language enters here, for some images are stimulated and enhanced by the sound of a word or the cadences of speech

e   Motor and haptic imagery may also be exploited, relating language, physical sensation and actions with implications not only for imagination but also for motor learning and control.

Who is to say that slow learners are incapable of these experiences or cannot gain from them? But that they need stimulation and the organization of 'process' situations leading to 'expressive' objectives few would deny; and is there any doubt that slow learners are more likely to enjoy and benefit from such experiences if their teachers are aware of the value of the experiences and consciously and positively build them into the language curriculum?

If these approaches to extending the language curriculum for slow learners are to be successful, then the teacher must keep in mind the characteristics of language capability summarized and well illustrated by Wilkinson.[18] Pupils should become aware of what language *is*, of what language *does*, and of the joys of language.

Another way of approaching the language curriculum is to view the use of language as skilled behaviour. Herriot[19] has discussed this approach in some detail. Here it is necessary only to indicate the qualities of skilled behaviour:

a   It is *hierarchical* – complete skills rest on underlying, essential sub-skills

b   It is *automatic* – through learning and practice, sequences of behaviour may be 'run off' efficiently without overt, conscious control

c   Skill involves *anticipation* – which itself rests on continuous monitoring and anticipation of outcomes, so that behaviour is modified, in process, to meet anticipated needs.

The association of the above qualities with the growth of language capability requires little elaboration, but effective application with slow learners calls for careful analysis of the language communication process. At this point the work of Argyle[20] is relevant. It is related not only to skill behaviour as outlined but also to the social interaction which *is* the communication process.

One analysis of the language–communication process is that provided by the *Illinois Test of Psycholinguistic Abilities*,[21] and programmes based on ITPA were observed in project schools. *Reading for Slow Learners* (pages 130–2) refers to work based upon the ITPA analysis, and in the discussion of readiness activities and remedial techniques it makes use of the ITPA approach. Here the reader is reminded of the main features of the analysis. Communication is seen as involving a *receptive* process of incoming signals and an *expressive* process which involves generation of signals. Intervening is an *organizing process* which is not directly observable. Specific measurement is made of *visual and auditory reception* and of *verbal and manual expression*. In the organizing process, *auditory–verbal association* assesses ability to relate spoken words, and *visual–manual association* the ability to relate visual symbols in a meaningful way with receptive–expressive language controlled. These functions are at a *representational level*, involving utilization of symbols which carry meaning. Other functions are measured at the *automatic level* where the individual's functioning is less voluntary but more organized and integrated. The main functions here are:

a *Closure*, grammatical, auditory and visual, which explore the ability to respond to or fill-in incomplete presentations of information

b *Sequential memory*, auditory and visual, which explore the ability to reproduce sequences involving short-term memory. Also included is a wide-ranging test of *sound blending*.

Results from the ITPA offer at least three possibilities:

a The teacher acquires insight into the pupil's strengths and weaknesses in the communication process as represented in the ITPA profile

b The contents of the sub-tests provide cues from which the teacher may develop process-related learning situations

c The contrast of visual–manual with auditory–vocal channels suggests ways in which the former (often relatively strong with slow learners) may be used to foster the latter (often the slow learner's weak area).

A similar analysis might be made using the Reynell Language Development Scale,[22] though this was not observed in project schools. To some degree these tests explore different aspects of communication, and together they could provide rich and stimulating information for classroom use. Similar use might be made of the Kephart-type motor development programmes, which are described in *Reading for Slow Learners* (chapter VIII). These concentrate on motor action, but there is emphasis on the relationship with speech and language in stimulating, regulating and shaping motor behaviour as well as in fostering the sequential language required to describe it. Other isolated approaches seen in project schools involve the use of programmed language material such as the *Peabody Language Development Kit*,[23] *Distar* language programme,[24] *Goal Programme*[25] and the development of the Rebus approach which is described in *Reading for Slow Learners*.[26]

The above approaches have at least two things in common: they are based upon skill analysis leading to the definition of specific objectives in pupil behaviour, and they involve a structured, repetitive approach to language skills which does not immediately commend itself to teachers in the schools of England and Wales. At present the use of these approaches is neither sufficiently widespread nor sufficiently controlled to allow proper evaluation. One reason for this is the limited involvement of school psychological services in the use and evaluation of these approaches in the work of the schools. Particularly penalized are approaches based upon ITPA, *Goal* (which is ITPA-derived) and possible developments based on Reynell. There is a need to bring teachers and educational psychologists together to explore these aspects of language learning so that teachers may acquire the insight into the tests from which they could develop programmes related to the test profiles of individual slow-learning pupils. Meanwhile, psychologists could establish base-lines, control teaching exposures, monitor pupil progress and seek some objective criteria as a basis for evaluation. There is a wide and important function here for co-operative in-service training of teachers and educational psychologists which, to be effective, should be both local and closely related to actual work with slow learners in the schools.

Resolving the language curriculum dichotomy

In most project schools the approach to language was, at least in theory, based upon experience plus stimulation, leading to assimilation of language capabilities. In one sense, and in the best examples, this closely resembled the process situation leading to expressive objectives. The approach is not unreasonable, given the lack of detailed information about the nature of language and the theoretical contradiction about its acquisition noted earlier, while it does meet major needs of the majority of pupils who are making normal school progress. But it has two important side-effects. It leads to a failure to identify pupils who are failing to progress, and it creates in teachers an antipathy to the more specific, repeated training and learning which slow-learning pupils may require.

Any resolution of the activity versus structured learning argument requires an acknowledgement that stimulating, varied, concrete experience clothed in appropriate language which reflects its qualities, is an essential background if slow learners are to gain from the specific, structured, repetitive learning situations which most of them need. Any school which has not achieved the former will gain little from the latter. But bring the two together and it may well be 'all systems go' for *all* the pupils. A further point is that carefully structured learning situations do not necessarily require programmed kits, though in certain circumstances these may bring great benefit .What is needed is a balanced approach by teachers, focused on the needs of slow learners and free from prejudices which usually are based on experience quite different fı om the experiences of the slow-learning pupil.

Once the school is established as an exciting, linguistically rich place of learning for the pupils, three requirements are imperative: the identification of pupils who are not progressing in language skills; the identification of the areas of language where pupils might benefit from structured learning; and the development of the necessary structured programmes.

In using a structured approach teachers have two main starting-points: the structure built into the materials and situations which they present to the pupils and upon and within which the pupils must operate; and the language which the teacher uses as she interacts with the pupils in the learning situations. Both require teacher skills, but the second makes greater demand upon teacher sensitivity. Given understanding of these basic facts, it is possible to enumerate certain generalizations which arise from observation of successful teaching with slow-learning pupils:

1 Language is most meaningful for slow learners when related to perceptual experience – to direct, sensory input from something which the pupil is *doing*.

2 For slow learners language learning is fostered by:

   a Refraining from direct instruction and asking questions which lead the pupil to insights or conclusions which are expressed in speech

   b Refraining from direct verbal corrections and substituting questions which lead the pupil to re-form his material or reformulate his response

   c Refraining from edict or command in controlling the pupil's attention and relying on comment, suggestion or question

   d Positively seeking verbal responses from the pupil upon which to base the next intervention by the teacher.

3 The foregoing closed or structured use of language must be balanced by open interaction:

   a By questions which encourage the pupil to elaborate his ideas or answers

   b By stimulating play with words, rhyme, verbal chains, alternatives, etc.

   c By encouraging divergent rather than convergent language and thought

   d By elaborating these situations through involving more pupils and, if possible, by the teacher's withdrawing from verbal intervention except to stimulate pupil interaction.

4 When using both closed and open approaches the teacher closely observes the pupil's language, especially his sequential structures or common grammatical forms. She should:

   a Be alert for emerging forms in the pupil's language and carefully arrange for their repetition and reinforcement

   b Feed in expansions of incomplete or immature forms in the pupil's speech, if possible shaping so that explanation is involved in addition to expansion

   c Operate on **b** as indicated in **a**

   d Ensure that in her language she presents pupils with a model of language relevant to their own but requiring aspiration as they reach towards it; this involves mature statements subsequently rephrased for the pupil but, if possible, involving him in question and explanation about the differences

   e If possible, anticipate in **d** forms which may be expected to emerge in the pupil's language as he interacts in learning situations

   f Utilize these techniques in both formal and informal situations.

5 Throughout all language activities and interactions the pupil should be encouraged to:

   a Classify objects on the basis of discrimination and generalization

   b Notice and perceive differences which determine exclusion in classifying activities

   c Generate concepts as a result of **a** and **b**

   d Deal with similar situations involving position in space, pattern, sequence, etc.

e Translate perceived situations into appropriate language statements

f Create concrete situations as defined in verbal descriptions

g Translate language sequences into motor actions

h Describe motor actions in language both simultaneously and subsequently

i Verbally describe anticipated movement from static diagrams or pictures

j Extend and elaborate the above situations as language capability improves.

6 The above activities do not exclude the reference aspects of language, for these involve the essential psychological processes of sensation and perception; but they go beyond them. Sensation and perception are used to foster imagery, imagination, concept formation, thought sequences, cause and effect, anticipation and insights – all expressed and handled in language which is an almost inseparable part of the fostering process. Meanwhile pupils should:

a Explore sensory qualities in the environment, extending and enriching perception of colour, shape, texture, movement, sound, objects, animals, people and places

b Develop judgement, appreciation, balance and control in their relationships with people, living creatures, natural life and the social, natural and material environment

c Express the qualities encountered in and arising from a and b in language which is increasingly appropriate, accurate and flexible

d At the same time use language to foster and express personal imagery arising from the experiences of a, b and c

e Become involved in the use of language in conceptual thinking and in convergent, problem-solving situations

f Extend growing facility with language to explore interpersonal relationships, acquire the ability to perceive situations from another person's point of view and express this in role-play, appreciation of literature and maturing of moral judgement and social understanding.

In developing these methodological approaches the teacher should understand that they imply generalized objectives which have many of the qualities of aims. They require translation into specific objectives related to the potentials of the slow learners with whom the teacher is to work. It is on this specific level that the *content* of learning situations for slow learners may diverge from those of their normal peers. Unless this is clearly understood teachers will consider that no different approach is required for slow learners, or argue that the above general objectives are beyond the capacities of slow learners; in either case continuing the common laissez-faire attitude to the slow-learner's language curriculum.

If successfully applied, the above suggestions should contribute positively to the many learning situations observed which, though perfectly acceptable and appropriate in general terms, lacked the internal clarity of objectives and structure required by many slow-learning pupils. But other changes in curriculum emphasis are also required.

1 The curriculum for slow learners should become more outward looking, exploring real situations outside the school and bringing into the classroom information, images, concepts, vocabulary, etc., which may be used in relevant classroom work.

2 In doing this, far more use should be made of reproducers (tape recorders, cameras, instant-picture cameras) to gain immediacy, stimulation and sensory inputs fostering imagery and imagination through the use of the techniques described in *Reading for Slow Learners* (pages 148–54).

3 To act in this way requires more pre-planning than was evident in most out-of-school sessions observed with slow learners. It requires:

a Detailed definition of the many learning objectives possible in each situation or experience to be presented to pupils

b Selection of the objectives to be exploited at the particular time of presentation

c Efficient anticipation of the aspects of the situation relevant to the selected objectives so that the actual photographs, recordings, etc., to be made can be identified, and so that there is prior introduction of the vocabulary and language required

d Careful thinking and planning for the continued exploitation of the outside experience in classwork involving picture displays, use of recordings, organization of slide–tape presentations, selection of work to be undertaken by pupils, etc., as well as the consideration of the shifting of classwork to other objectives inherent in the experience and its records

e The recording of the learning which pupils have acquired in terms of information, concepts and language in order to facilitate later reinforcement, shifts as indicated in **d**, and for the benefit of subsequent teachers.

4 In addition to the above points, each situation or experience should be linked, where possible, with wider aspects of curricula, with local and national affairs or even, by contrast, with situations in other countries or other historical times. Use should be made of literature, including poetry or drama where appropriate. The objective of this is not to overload the slow learner with detailed learning, for that can be unproductive, but to exploit awareness, widen background and give richness to the experience which will motivate learning in those detailed aspects required if selected objectives are to be achieved.

It was the general precision of approach suggested in the above comments which was absent from the language curriculum in the less successful schools, and might further improve most of those considered more successful with their slow learners. The precision was noticeable in the work with language programmes where this was observed. The above suggestions are designed to indicate how features of the precision may be introduced into open language activities with slow learners which, if carefully organized and presented, should have the advantages of relevance, interest and motivation for the pupil. The other advantages of the language programmes, repetition and reinforcement, rest within the skill of individual teachers, though the above suggestions should lead to clarity of objectives which could make both easier to achieve in open, active, teaching–learning situations. And this is what slow learners need if their language is to be enriched and improved.

Summary

In summarizing, how can one encompass such a complete process as language, about which so little is positively known and so much tentative and contradictory, when the concern is for those who teach and learn in schools and are unable to stop and await more positive leads from the 'experts'? Certainly the lack of precision in the language curriculum for slow learners cannot be made the sole responsibility of teachers. Conversely, the more successful curricula rest upon the organization of general language experiences which have the quality of process situations from which acceptable expressive objectives emerge. It appears that about half the schools approach success on this basis but all would gain from more careful analysis of functions of language other than the referential. More attention is required to language as regulating personal behaviour, influencing the behaviour of others and as the vehicle for interpersonal interaction. Language in relation to thought, imagery and imagination also requires more attention. Special efforts are called for to identify pupils who fail to respond to the situational approach, to define their specific needs and to develop specific structured learning programmes relevant to their needs. In doing this there should be close collaboration between teachers and educational psychologists using existing measures of language function as the basis for classroom language programmes. Such collaboration should be fostered by local in-service training related to slow learners in the schools. An attempt has been made to show how the teacher may introduce necessary structure into open language activities without the use of language kits, though these have their place and value. No attempt is made to describe the wider aims of language across the curriculum, as the aims of *A Language for Life*[27] are accepted as relevant for slow learners and contributing to the concept of a common curriculum. It is noted, however, that there is much to do in translating the aims of *A Language for Life* into pupil behavioural objectives. It is at this point that the special needs of slow learners will become paramount and relevant questions have been posed. Here, the contribution of experienced teachers of slow learners in the formulation of LEA language programmes is seen as essential if slow learners are to receive the consideration which is necessary to improve their language curriculum in both extent and quality.

References

1. W. K. BRENNAN, *Reading for Slow Learners: a Curriculum Guide.* Schools Council Curriculum Bulletin 7. Evans/Methuen Educational, 1978.
2. D. LAWTON, 'Preparation for changes in the curriculum', in J. W. Tibble (ed.), *The Extra Year.* Routledge & Kegan Paul, 1970.
3. R. GOLDMAN, *Religious Thinking from Childhood to Adolescence.* Routledge & Kegan Paul, 1964.
4. L. KOHLBERG, 'The development of children's orientation towards a moral order', *Vita Humana*, Parts 6 and 9. 1963. 'Moral education in the schools: a developmental view', *School Review*, **74**, 1966, 1–30. R. BROWN, *Social Psychology.* Collier Macmillan, 1965. W. KAY, *Moral Development.* Allen & Unwin, 1968. J. WILSON, N.

WILLIAMS and B. SUGARMAN, *Introduction to Moral Education*. Penguin Books, 1967. N. J. BULL, *Moral Judgement from Childhood to Adolescence*. Routledge & Kegan Paul, 1969. R. F. PECK, R. J. HAVINGHURST, R. COOPER, J. LILIENTHAL and D. MORE, *The Psychology of Character Development*. John Wiley, New York, 1964. J. PIAGET, *The Moral Judgement of the Child*. Routledge & Kegan Paul, 1932. W. R. NIBLETT (ed.), *Moral Education in a Changing Society*. Faber, 1963. G. GRAHAM, *Moral Learning and Development, Theory and Research*. Batsford, 1972.

5. R. GULLIFORD and P. WIDLAKE, *Teaching Materials for Disadvantaged Children*, Schools Council Curriculum Bulletin 5. Evans/Methuen Educational, 1974.

6. GULLIFORD and WIDLAKE, *Teaching Materials for Disadvantaged Children*.

7. PIAGET, *The Moral Judgement of the Child*. GOLDMAN, *Religious Thinking from Childhood to Adolescence*.

8. M. ARGYLE, *Human Interaction*. Methuen, 1969. *The Psychology of Interpersonal Behaviour*. Penguin Books, 2nd edn, 1972. *Bodily Communication*. Methuen, 1975. 'Personality and social behaviour', in R. Harré (ed.), *Personality*. Blackwell, Oxford, 1977.

9. Nuffield Primary Mathematics Project (1964–71): materials published by W. & R. Chambers and John Murray; Midlands Mathematics Experiment (1961–   ): materials published by Harrap; Schools Council Mathematics for the Majority Project (1967–72): teacher's guides published by Chatto & Windus Educational; Schools Council Mathematics for the Majority Continuation Project (1971–75): pupil material published by Schofield & Sims; SMILE (Secondary Mathematics Individualized Learning Experiment) (1972–   ): materials from ILEA Learning Materials Service.

10. GULLIFORD and WIDLAKE, *Teaching Materials for Disdavantaged Children*.

11. Nuffield Junior Science Project (1964–66): materials published by Collins; Schools Council Nuffield Science 5–13 Project (1967–75); materials published by Macdonald Educational; Nuffield Secondary Science Project (1965–70): materials published by Longman Group. (An evaluation of both Science 5–13 and Nuffield Secondary Science has been published in the Schools Council Research Studies Series: WYNNE HARLEN, *Science 5–13: a Formative Evaluation*, Macmillan Education, 1975, and DOROTHY J. ALEXANDER, *Nuffield Secondary Science: an Evaluation*, Macmillan Education, 1974.)

12. J. S. BRUNER, *Man: a Course of Studies*, Guide to the Course. Education Development Centre, Cambridge, Mass., 1969.

13. W. K. BRENNAN, *Shaping the Education of Slow Learners*. Routledge & Kegan Paul, 1974.

14. J. WILSON, *A Study of the Occupational Adjustment of Backward Boys and Girls*. M.Ed. thesis, University of Leicester, 1971.

15. Department of Education and Science, *A Language for Life* (Bullock Report). HMSO, 1975.

16. Department of Education and Science, *A Language for Life* (Bullock Report).

17. P. HERRIOT, *An Introduction to the Psychology of Language*. Methuen, 1970. M. A. K. HALLIDAY, 'Relevant models of language', in A. M. Wilkinson (ed.), *The State of Language*. University of Birmingham School of Education, 1969. A. M. WILKINSON, *The Foundations of Language*. Oxford University Press, 1971.

18. WILKINSON, *The Foundations of Language*.

19. HERRIOT, *An Introduction to the Psychology of Language*.

20. ARGYLE, *Human Interaction: The Psychology of Interpersonal Behaviour*.

21. S. A. KIRK, J. J. MCCARTHY and W. D. KIRK, *Illinois Test of Psycholinguistic Abilities*. University of Illinois Press, Urbana, Illinois, 1968 (distributed in UK by National Foundation for Educational Research).

22. J. REYNELL, *Infant and Young Children's Language Scales*. NFER Publishing, Windsor, 1969.

23. LLOYD DUNN, J. O. SMITH and KATHRYN HORTON, *Peabody Language Development Kit*. American Guidance Services, Minnesota, 1968. (Distributed in UK by Educational Evaluation Enterprises, Bristol, and NFER Publishing, Windsor.)

24. SIEGFRIED ENGELMANN and JEAN OSBORN, *Distar Language*. Science Research Associates, Henley-on-Thames, 1969.

25. M. B. KARNES, *Guide to the Goal Programme: Language Development*. Milton Bradley, Springfield, Mass., 1972. (Available from Learning Development Aids, Wisbech.)

26. R. W. WOODCOCK, *The Peabody Rebus Reading Program*. 3 vols. American Guidance Services, Minnesota, 1967. BRENNAN, *Reading for Slow Learners*, chapter XIV. See also videotape 5 in the series, *Teaching the Slow Learner*, produced by the Inner London Education Authority Television Service.

27. Department of Education and Science, *A Language for Life* (Bullock Report).

VII. Curricular needs of slow learners

Previous chapters have described the project schools and indicated the shape and quality of curricula observed in them during the work of the project. This chapter brings together the results of the experience gained in the schools, attempting to relate it to the problem of improving the quality of education offered to slow-learning pupils.

Classification and the curriculum

A common approach to the classification of slow learners operated on a bipolar basis. It consisted of making a distinction between pupils who were 'dull' and those who were 'remedial'. Dull pupils were those who had low scores on intelligence tests, or who had demonstrated prolonged failure in acquiring simple skills or knowledge known to be mastered by younger children. Remedial pupils were those with intelligence-test scores within (or near) normal limits, whose general competence was normal for their age but who had great difficulty with classroom learning, usually with reading. In many project schools the distinction between the above groups still rested on comparisons between mental age and achievement age in the form of an achievement quotient, notwithstanding the fact that this procedure has been shown to be of doubtful validity.

In curriculum terms the distinction was equally simple. The dull group required some special provision across the curriculum, possibly throughout the whole of their school life; their learning, it was assumed, would always be restricted and behind that of their normal age peers. Remedial pupils required the temporary support of special teaching in reading which would enable them to make up their deficiencies so that they could join the normal classes in the school. Usually this teaching was provided on a withdrawal basis, the pupils remaining members of an appropriate school class. What was remarkable in the schools was the way these groups were mutually exclusive in terms of their curricular needs. The dull were rarely found to have remedial needs, while the remedials were rarely dull. And this distinction struck deeply. Specific learning disabilities, perceptual inadequacies, motor difficulties or neurological impairment appeared to be regarded as more interesting in remedial pupils of normal potential. Even in special schools, where all pupils were regarded as dull, and where the general curriculum was admirably suited to their needs, the attention given to the above specific learning disabilities was usually less than adequate. In many LEAs the above distinction is still regarded as the proper one in deciding between special school (for the dull) or ordinary school (for the remedials).

In a minority of the schools both groups were recognized and attempts made to provide appropriate curricula for both. More frequently, however, one group had been recognized and provided for in the belief that the whole problem of slow learners was thereby resolved. In all the schools there is need for more careful consideration of the different curricular needs in the population of slow learners and for a new approach to the classification of needs in a way which will assist thinking about curricular provision. On the basis of such a classification teachers could make decisions about differentiated curricula, assemble the materials required to implement them, acquire the teaching skills essential for success, and define the objectives which would identify that success. The process which serves to identify and classify the needs determining the differentiated curricula will also serve to identify pupil needs, not only between different pupils but within individual pupils. Once the school is aware of different needs in slow learners and has assembled the facilities to meet them, then the problem becomes one of matching curricular resources to the curricular needs of the pupils; the instrument for this is the timetable which brings together groups with similar needs and is individualized as and when necessary.

A classification of pupil needs based upon the above principles proved helpful during the work of the project and contributed to the evaluation of curricula observed in the project schools. The classification results in three main types of pupils' needs which require, respectively, adaptive-developmental curriculum; corrective or compensatory curriculum; and remedial curriculum. There is discussion of the model in the literature[1] and in the first of the series of videotapes, *Teaching the Slow Learner*.[2] Here it serves to give point to the general principles noted above.

ADAPTIVE-DEVELOPMENTAL CURRICULUM

The pupil needs which indicate an adaptive-developmental curriculum are varied and extensive, affect many aspects of behaviour in addition to learning in school, and have about them some indication of permanence.

The needs are such that, seen in relation to current knowledge and available educational techniques, they appear to require special adaptation of the normal school curriculum from the beginning and all through formal education. In addition, it may be necessary to modify normal teaching methods, and even school organization, in order to meet these needs both appropriately and efficiently. For some pupils appropriateness and efficiency may be attainable only in a special school. But the adaptation required must not be static. The pupil's needs are *special* but they also change as the pupil develops and matures. Consequently, the curriculum must develop, at least to keep pace with the changing needs of the pupil; better, in anticipation of those needs in order to meet them efficiently; at best to *create* pupil needs which will provide motivation for a wider and richer curriculum. Of course, all education should be adaptive and developmental in this sense. The importance of these concepts for slow learners is that their application requires much more deliberate, planned intervention by the teacher than would be either necessary or desirable with normal pupils.

Certain circumstances are associated with slow learners who need adaptive-developmental curricula (they are not necessarily mentioned in order of importance): low level of intellectual competence; gross perceptual immaturity; restricted language; marked personal and social immaturity; difficulty with concept formation; difficulty with sequential thought; extreme difficulty in establishing new knowledge or skills; severe difficulty with learning in basic school subjects; low level of general awareness; and continually shifting attention and interest. Only slow learners with the most extreme disabilities exhibit all the above features. Among the rest there is a wide variety of combinations and equal variation in the level of severity. That is why intimate knowledge of the pupil is so important in making decisions about adaptive-developmental needs.

It will be obvious from the discussion so far that an adaptive-developmental curriculum is concerned with the whole education of those pupils for whom it is necessary. The objectives are long-term objectives which make severe demands on curriculum planning. Teachers involved in the planning have three bases from which they must work: first, intimate knowledge of the pupil; secondly, equally intimate knowledge of the pupil's family, neighbourhood and social circumstances likely to affect his attitude to school and learning; thirdly, some anticipation of the kinds of demand which the pupil is likely to meet as a young adult faced with earning a living and supporting a family, and in experiencing some satisfaction from his life. It is from these sources that teachers derive the information which allows them to generate the objectives of an appropriate and balanced adaptive-developmental curriculum.

CORRECTIVE OR COMPENSATORY CURRICULUM

The pupil needs which make necessary a corrective curriculum may be regarded as being the result of limitations of environment which create *learning difficulties* for the pupil. Absence of critical, early experience necessary to support normal learning, or gaps in basic knowledge or skill required for normal school progress, seriously affect language, reading and number skills in particular. Usually the inadequacies do not operate over the whole of the pupil's learning. Close examination of the retardation shows that it is caused by specific gaps in experience, knowledge or skill which are the real obstacles to normal progress. An exception to this is where environmental deprivation has been massive and unresolved from early years: then the child's intellectual development may have been affected in a way which is not yet fully understood but which creates needs more appropriately met through the adaptive-developmental curriculum. For most pupils, however, corrective teaching, or compensatory experiences which are carefully designed and efficiently executed, meet the specific needs, close the gaps and bring learning progress to an acceptable level.

Circumstances associated with slow learners who require corrective or compensatory curricula are as follows (again not necessarily in order of importance): general absence of intellectually stimulating adults in the child's background; background of restricted experience; inadequate language model in the home; unconcern about education in the home; inability of parents to assist learning; lack of reading matter in the home and limited reading by adults for children; homes which over-value physical strength and skill; restricted, unstimulating neighbourhood; absences from school; and inappropriate or ineffective teaching in school. In some way the above circumstances seem to cluster in the backgrounds of pupils who need corrective education, though there is wide variation in the kind and severity of the specific learning difficulties generated by them.

The specific objectives of a corrective or compensatory curriculum can be specified with reasonable accuracy and are attainable over short- or medium-term time-scales. The objectives do not constitute the whole of the pupil's education, but they are more easily achieved where the general curriculum which the pupil is following is exciting, stimulating and generates good motivation for learning. Consequently the specific teaching which the pupil requires may be planned into the general class programme. Where that is not possible, or is inappropriate, then specific teaching in corrective curricula may be organized on a withdrawal basis, though it is important that the pupil should not be out of his class or group for more than the minimum of time required to achieve the specific prescribed objectives. One remarkable thing about successful corrective curricula is that they succeed without special techniques, on the basis of sound, traditional primary methods, carefully adapted to the pupil's needs, shaped to the specified gaps to be filled, in circumstances which allow the teacher to give the attention required by educationally disadvantaged pupils. These curricula are corrective when they are eliminating inaccurate or inappropriate learning and replacing it by learning which is accurate, appropriate and permanent. They are compensatory when the objective is to establish knowledge, skill or experience necessary to eliminate gaps in early learning which create learning difficulties for the pupil. It should be noted here that though curricular objectives and content are derived from the study of individual pupils, it is usually possible to organize corrective or compensatory teaching by bringing together small groups of pupils with similar curricular needs.

REMEDIAL CURRICULUM

The remedial curriculum described here is intended to meet pupil needs which were not widely recognized in the project schools. The needs are not those which arise from environmental inadequacy or deprivation of experience in the pupil's history, though for some pupils these may be complicating secondary factors. On the contrary, the needs are most easily recognized in pupils of normal intellectual potential who live in circumstances richly conducive to normal learning but who fail to learn, or are retarded in a way incompatible with their potential and circumstances. The learning failure of these pupils may be regarded as arising from *learning disabilities* which are within the pupil. The hypothesis is that the disabilities arise from structural or functional inadequacy or abnormality in the neurological systems which conduct sensory information to the central nervous system, in the storage of information in the system, or in the recall of information as the basis of learning and behaviour.

Certain features may be noted in pupils who require remedial curricula (they are not necessarily given in order of importance or frequency): minor but critical features of motor development (general clumsiness, immature fine motor control); perceptual disorders (background–foreground confusion, difficulty in part–whole discrimination); difficulty with perceptual-motor links (hand–eye co-ordination); abnormalities in classification of objects (by bizarre, illogical or insignificant features);

confused thought processes (perseverance, illogical gaps, bizarre solutions to problems); abnormality in motor behaviour (hyperactivity, persistent repetition); specific language difficulties (reversals, hesitations, repetiton of words or phrases); specific difficulties with written, printed or graphic material (matching, copying, tracing, writing, reading); specific difficulty with numbers (reversals, inversions, omissions, column displacement, confusion of cardinal and ordinal function); specific nervous-system functional difficulties (short- and/or long-term memory, abnormal fixation of attention and interest, distractability, minor tics or obsessional behaviour patterns). Many different combinations of these features appear in pupils who require remedial education. The pattern of the features often changes for the same pupil while for others the features appear intermittently. It should also be noted that widespread and consistent breakdown or inadequacy in nervous-system functions creates needs which are probably better classified and dealt with as described for adaptive-developmental education.

At present remedial curricula (in the precise form discussed here) are only beginning to emerge in the schools, a fact which makes it difficult to generalize about them. Their tentative and experimental nature has been noted (page 99) with some evaluation of their effectiveness; there is comment on content (pages 72–3); on recording (pages 78–9); and the relation of these to objectives (pages 83–4). Wedell[3] has provided an excellent summary and evaluation of the current status of these approaches to learning disabilities. Gulliford[4] has indicated the value of the approaches and the concepts on which they are based while warning about the danger of assuming a neurological cause for learning difficulties on the sole evidence of classroom observation. There is certainly a strong case for developing work on remedial curricula, particularly in the very early stages of education, and though a high degree of one-to-one teacher–pupil work is required in contemporary approaches, there should be some attempt to develop small-group techniques for pupils with similar needs.

Classification of need and the teacher

It is stressed again that the above classification is based upon an analysis of curricular needs found among slow-learning pupils; it does not identify individual pupils. Some slow learners will have needs which will require the use of all three curricula. Most of the pupils following adaptive-developmental curricula will be found to require corrective or compensatory curricula and some will require remedial curricula as well.

Other pupils, following remedial curricula, may miss out on the wider, richer aspects of primary-school curricula in a way which may subsequently require corrective or compensatory curricula. Curricular failure cannot be ruled out and may change the nature of the pupil's needs. Thus the failure of corrective or remedial curricula may leave a pupil with unresolved, permanent needs which will require adaptive-developmental curricula designed to meet them. The identified needs also affect pupils at different levels of severity and this should be reflected in teaching proposals. Some needs might be met through appropriate advice given to the pupil's class teacher; others may require the provision of a special programme to be carried out in class by the classroom teacher; at another level, teaching in class by a specialist teacher may be necessary. Then there are the withdrawal techniques where the frequency and duration of out-of-class time vary to match the pupil's needs. For some pupils, especially those requiring adaptive-developmental curricula, a full-time special class may be necessary. A small minority of slow learners may require modifications of curricula, teaching and support which can be provided only in a special school. In determining the situation required to meet the pupil's needs, the medical or social aspects of the pupil's needs may be of little relevance – a fact which colleagues in those disciplines do not always understand. The critical factor is the kind of curriculum and teaching required by the pupil and the situation in which it can be provided efficiently – the objective being to create the situation as near as possible to the normal, mainstream classroom situation.

The above approach to the curricular needs of slow learners is absolutely dependent on the identification of the pupil's needs. Just how such needs are to be identified is a question frequently posed by teachers in discussions. There is no easy answer. Standardized tests of intellectual function, attainments and social competence provide normative data. Diagnostic assessments of sub-skills provide insights into patterns of competence and highlight gaps in knowledge or skill. Specialized techniques are emerging which do the same for perception, patterns of thinking and language. Criterion-based assessment of pupil behaviour from teachers who know the pupils well, though subjective, adds another important dimension. But the critical process is evaluation – the consideration of the total information by a well-trained, experienced teacher of slow learners, or by an educational adviser or educational psychologist who has relevant experience with such pupils and has seen the pupil who is being assessed. What is essential is the combination of technical expertise in making use of normative and criterion-based measures allied to the kind of experience necessary to make use of *teaching* information from the classroom. The latter will become more important as the realization grows that the teaching situation represents the richest possible source of diagnostic information leading to important insights into the curricular and teaching needs of slow-learning pupils. Many teachers of slow learners accept the importance of the kind of development described, but they protest that they lack the training that would allow them to use their experience in this way, and they may well be correct in this. If so, then a critical area for in-service education has been identified which should be taken up and developed in LEAs and in advanced courses in special education. There may also be a case for bringing together teachers, psychologists and advisers for this kind of advanced training.

Why curricula for slow learners?

This is not an academic or hypothetical question, but one frequently posed by teachers of slow learners in the project schools. It is essential that there should be a rational answer to the question, for a sizable minority of teachers find the idea of organized curricula for slow learners difficult to accept, and some find it totally unacceptable.

There are at least eight reasons for developing well-organized curricula for slow learners in the schools:

1 It is impossible for any school to teach, or for any pupil to learn, all the things that would benefit the pupil – at least during the statutory period of education. This remains true even if allowance is made for incidental learning both within and outside school through the 'hidden curriculum' of life. It follows that whatever is taught and learned in school represents only a small part of all that *might* be learned. What is important, especially for pupils with learning difficulties, is that what the school requires the pupil to learn should bear some relationship to his present and future needs. In other words, the selection of the learning experiences to be presented to the pupil should rest on a system of priorities.

2 Slow learners, by definition, find learning a slow, frustrating and difficult process. They require more presentations, more repetitions and more reinforcement than their 'normal' peers if their learning is to be accurate and permanent. They do not easily acquire insight, relate different aspects of learning or generalize established learning in new situations. They need more teacher intervention and help. As a

result, time presses heavily on their teachers, reducing what can be learned during the years at school. The selection of relevant learning for the pupil thus becomes even more critical, adding to the reasons for having a rational curriculum, and emphasizing the need to make it efficient.

3 Pupils need continuity in learning. Slow learners move between classes, most move between schools and some move from one part of the country to another. And even if the pupil stays put, teachers move. Other pupils are absent through illness, accident, etc., and require assistance on return if they are not to fall even further behind. The existence of organized curricula, properly recorded, reduces the negative effect of these circumstances by enabling teachers to build on the pupils' educational experience and identify and arrange any additional teaching which may be required.

4 A well-organized mainstream curriculum for slow learners is both a means of identifying pupils who require its modification and a starting-point for such modification. There is much talk in the schools about 'modifying the curriculum for slow learners'. This is a perfectly proper approach, but the idea implies that there is an existing curriculum to be modified and that there is a clear objective to guide the modifications – in this case, identified special needs of the pupil. Failure on the main curriculum can identify a pupil's special needs and become the growing-point for the modified curriculum suggested by the failure. The relationship between main and modified curricula is discussed in detail in connexion with reading in *Reading for Slow Learners*.

5 A good curriculum assists the pupil. The clarity which it confers on teachers helps them to give slow learners insight into their own educational progress so that they have some grasp of where they are, and where they are supposed to be going. This kind of involvement is pregnant with opportunities for improved motivation and, with senior pupils, for self-evaluation.

6 The curricula offer support to the teachers in the school. Given good, well-organized curricula, they can feel more confident about providing additions, substitutions, alternatives or modifications for pupils who require them and, if the curriculum is seen in a proper context (to be discussed below), then its support liberates the teacher to act creatively and confidently where only she can act – at the point of classroom teaching and learning.

7 Good curricula aid communication with parents. They clarify the minds of teachers about the selected objectives, their relationship to aims and methods and the evaluation of outcomes. All this helps teachers in their task of ensuring that parents are aware of the purposes of the school and understand the supportive contribution which they can make to assist their children.

8 Similar considerations apply to relations between school and community. A school which has thought out its aims, objectives, methods and means of evaluation is in a good position to explain its work with slow learners to the community it serves, create wider understanding of slow-learning pupils and ensure that community evaluations of such pupils are relevant, realistic and rational.

A majority of teachers with whom the project team discussed this subject feared that organized curricula for slow learners could lead to a loss of professional freedom. There is no mistaking the anxieties generated here. These anxieties are not unfounded. As the discussion of the shape of the curriculum has shown (Chapter V), the current curricula for slow learners are heavily biased towards content which, though laid down by the headteacher rather than by an examination board, may be regarded as just as restrictive by individual teachers. In the curricular documents submitted to the project the bias is unmistakable. Almost every curriculum consists of a catalogue of contents, a list of things to be taught by teachers and learned by pupils, the whole subdivided into class or year sections within which content is listed according to the chosen organization (subject, topic, centre of interest, etc.). They can be formidable documents! Even more formidable are the curricula which spell out the methods to be adopted by teachers. Indeed, though this may seem a harsh judgement, most of the curricula presented to the project are reminiscent of the old-style syllabus, and show little evidence of more recent thinking about the nature of the curriculum. The degree of content prescription in the submissions from schools contrasts with the anxieties expressed about the curriculum.

There are two main inferences to be drawn from the situation just described. First, there may be justification for the anxiety expressed by many teachers and undoubtedly shared by others, especially if the curriculum were to become 'centralized'. Secondly, there is some kind of educational 'cultural lag' at work, as a result of which teachers of slow learners, once in the vanguard of innovation, are being left behind by advances in educational thinking and practice about the nature of curricula. If this is so, then it identifies a critical task for the in-service education of teachers of slow learners, and particularly for headteachers and others who have most direct influence on curricula in the schools. However that may be, referring back to the discussion in Chapter V, it can be seen that curricula which are strong on aims and content but wanting in concern with objectives, and in the recording and evaluation which follows from that concern, are unlikely to possess the sharpness or edge necessary if slow learners are to be efficiently educated. To some extent this is confirmed by the discussion of curricular quality in Chapter VI. There is, therefore, a great need to tighten the curriculum, to specify objectives and to evaluate much more carefully the extent and efficiency with which they are achieved. But will not this tightening, this control, further restrict the freedom of teachers and add to the anxieties noted above? This question also was posed in discussion with teachers in project schools and, like the other questions, requires an answer. The answer is 'Yes'. The control will act as a constraint upon the teacher unless an approach to the curriculum can be devised which produces the control and efficiency increasingly demanded by parents and by the community while safeguarding the right of the teacher to exercise professional skills as freely as possible in the interest of the slow-learning pupils. This dichotomy has been the central dilemma facing a project team striving to reach some conclusions about the curriculum for slow learners. How can the two requirements be reconciled?

Parents, community and the school curriculum

It must be said at once that the problem posed above is proper and relevant, deriving directly from the practical situation involving the schools and the community. Parents and other adults in the community *do* know about the kinds of demands which will face slow learners as adults; they *do* have shrewd ideas, based upon their own experience, of the knowledge, skills, attitudes, etc., likely to assist slow learners in meeting the demands; and they *do* meet the bills which keep the whole system of education in existence. Like all paying customers of a service they *do* have the right to value for money as *they* see it. What parents and other adults do *not* know about are the nature and complexity of the difficulties which slow learners face in school, the relationship of these to personality, family background, social status, interests, patterns of motivation, etc., and the changes among these variables which perplex teachers of slow learners. Knowledge of these is part of the professional equipment of the teacher. And if the teacher is a teacher of slow learners, then the exercise of the professional function depends on the possession of the essential knowledge about the pupil and his circumstances at a level so intimate that it is unlikely to exist outside the classroom, and certainly does not exist outside the school. If the curriculum for slow learners is to be relevant, realistic and rational, then critical decisions about it must be made at points where the intimacy of knowledge referred to above can influence the decisions – that is, within the school and, better, within the classroom. Indeed, the real nature of the professional freedom of the teacher resides in her involvement in these intimate decisions in school and classroom. But in admitting this it should be noted that the question of whether or not the curriculum is real might be better answered by parents and other adults in the community who may also have an important contribution to make on the question of its relevance for slow learners. Seen in this way, it is possible to suggest how the involvement of parents and the community in the curriculum may be reconciled with the freedom of the teacher in the school; though this requires a view of the nature of the curriculum rarely met in the curricular documents or in discussion with teachers in the project schools.

A curriculum of involvements and objectives

In order to resolve the above problem fully, the first essential is to move the schools away from their current concern with the details of content as the main part of the curriculum and to persuade them that the curriculum should be more concerned with objectives. There are other good reasons for such a move, of course, but for present purposes it is sufficient to note that as long as schools concentrate on content it is impossible for the community or parents to become involved without creating tensions about the freedom of teachers. The outline of a suggested scheme for the development of involvement in curricula is set out in Table 8. The first column indicates the section of the curriculum being considered, the second column indicates the partner taking the lead, and the third column, the other contributing partners. It is assumed that the community is represented through the local education authority and this for two main reasons. First, the local community has many factions with differing opinions and it is necessary that these should be reconciled into some sort of community view. The LEA, as part of the elected local government which also has the power to co-opt members to secure wide representation, and to arrange community representation among school managers or governors, is well situated to reflect a community point of view. Secondly, the LEA is the body charged by Parliament to provide education in its locality and it must, therefore, remain in overall control of the local system of education. It is assumed that there will be parent representatives among school managers or governors, but in addition it is assumed that there will be a body of parents of pupils in the school, meeting regularly, discussing school problems with the teachers and in a position to communicate with school managers or governors and members of the LEA. It would also help if there were a requirement from central government that each LEA must make special arrangements to meet the needs of its slow learners in consultation with the schools, parents and the community, so that provision for slow learners becomes a positive requirement of the system. In visualizing the operation of curriculum involvement as suggested in Table 8, it is assumed that consultation and interaction among the partners would be more frequent than with 'normal' pupils because of the greater heterogeneity of slow learners, the need to adapt to changes in the school population, and the need for consultations between teachers and individual parents about the modified curriculum or altered teaching patterns for individual pupils.

The table suggests wide involvement of the partners in selecting the aims which will shape and guide the curriculum for slow learners in a way consistent with values accorded importance by the community. The translation of the aims into terminal objectives for pupils is a professional task for teachers and LEA advisers, though there is a need to make use of community experience. Selection of intermediate objectives is a fully professional task for teachers and LEA advisers. Scrutiny of the conclusions of the professionals is opened out for comment to parents and the community. Note, though, that the selection, organization and presentation of the specific learning experiences, through which pupils are to attain their curricular objectives, are the concern of the classroom teacher with the involvement of the headteacher for advice and as the arbiter of essential continuity in the school. However, the scrutiny of learning objectives is for the headteacher and LEA advisers, in order to secure an objectivity made impossible for the class teacher by the intimacy she must establish with pupils if she is to perform her role effectively. Control of pupil learning passes back firmly into the hands of the class teacher with professional support available if required. Evaluation of curriculum outcomes passes again more widely to the partners who are able to make use of experience and insight based upon industrial and commercial situations unlikely to have been experienced by teachers but which will face slow learners when they leave school. Feedback repeats the pattern with wide involvement in modification of aims and terminal objectives but increasing professional control for modification of intermediate objectives and learning experiences.

Table 8 Curriculum involvement: teachers, school governors, parents and LEA

Curricular area	Lead partner	Contributing partners
1 Aims	LEA	Teachers Governors Parents
2 Selection of terminal objectives	Teachers Headteacher	LEA Governors Parents
3 Determination of intermediate objectives	Teachers Headteacher	LEA
4 Scrutiny of objectives:		
Real?	LEA	Governors Parents
Relevant?	LEA	Governors Parents
Realistic?	Teachers	LEA Parents
Rational?	Teachers	LEA
5 Learning experiences:		
Selection of content	Class teachers	Headteacher
Organization of experiences	Class teachers	Headteacher
Presentation of experiences	Class teachers	Headteacher
Scrutiny of experiences	Headteacher	LEA
6 Control of pupil learning:		
Recording	Class teacher	Headteacher LEA
Measurement/assessment	Class teacher	Headteacher LEA
Evaluation	Class teacher	Headteacher LEA
7 Evaluation of curriculum outcomes:		
Real?	LEA	Governors Parents
Relevant?	LEA	Governors Parents
Efficient?	LEA	Governors
8 Feedback:		
Modification of aims	LEA	Teachers Governors Parents
Modification of objectives:		
terminal	Teachers Headteacher	LEA Governors Parents
intermediate	Teachers Headteacher	LEA
Modification of learning experiences	Class teachers	Headteacher

There are a number of points to be noted about these suggestions for curriculum involvement. First, they *are* only suggestions intended to promote thought and discussion. Secondly, they are intended to bring the parents and the community into closer interaction with the school, not only for what they can contribute, but so that the schools may have increased opportunity to inform the others of their work and secure increased understanding and acceptance of slow-learning pupils. Thirdly, the stress is on education, teaching and objectives involving knowledge, skills and cognitive processes. Concern for the *welfare* of slow learners is well established in the schools, in danger of ousting the above educational objectives, and the balance needs to be redressed. Fourthly, it should be noted that the partners may all be involved in the curriculum without full benefit if the current laissez-faire attitude to curriculum is maintained. Fifthly, it is repeated that there is an urgent need for changed attitudes to the curriculum in the schools if teachers of slow learners are to welcome and accept the wider involvements in a creative manner.

A curriculum which stops at the classroom door

It is important that teachers of slow learners should understand clearly the nature of a curriculum which combines wide community involvement with an emphasis on the objectives to be pursued in the education of slow learners. Unlike most of what passes for curricula at present, the objectives curricula does *not* spell out the detail of what the teacher must teach to her pupils. Nor, except in the broadest manner necessary to ensure continuity in the school, does the objectives curriculum specify the detail of *how* the pupils are to be taught. What the objectives curriculum does spell out, with a clarity limited only by the competence of those who develop it, are first, the aims which are to shape the education of slow learners, and secondly, the behavioural objectives which it is believed the pupils should achieve if the aims of their education are to be satisfied. In arriving at aims and objectives the collective experience of the community is harnessed in the task. Within the school, professional teachers translate the terminal objectives into intermediate objectives consistent with the development of slow-learning pupils, the general organization of the teaching groups or classes in the school and the common view of curriculum method which represents a consensus of the views of the teaching staff. Also included here is the description of essential experiences and situations to which pupils should be exposed in order to promote the emergence of the 'expressive' or 'value' objectives difficult or impossible to specify in behavioural terms. From this professional process intermediate objectives are allocated to appropriate levels, classes or teaching groups. At this point the curriculum stops – hence the heading, 'A curriculum which stops at the classroom door'.

The purpose of the objectives curriculum at this point is clear: it is to ensure that the teacher enters the classroom as fully prepared as possible to pursue the objectives of the phase of pupil learning for which she is responsible. If this is to be accomplished the teacher must have the following competencies:

1 Clear understanding of the objectives which pupils should attain in the learning for which there is teacher responsibility

2 Awareness of how such objectives follow from previous teaching and relate to behavioural objectives achieved by the pupils

3 Awareness of how current objectives are related to, and prepare for, objectives to be achieved by pupils later in the curriculum

4 Understanding of the overall pattern of terminal and intermediate objectives which, together with critical expressive situations, constitute the body of the school curriculum

5 Clarity of concepts about the general approach to method in the school, its importance for continuity of learning and its value in contributing to expressive objectives in the curriculum

6 Awareness of the teacher's responsibility for the selection, organization and presentation of learning experiences through which pupils are to attain their immediate objectives

7 Awareness of the teacher's responsibility for recording, measuring, assessing and evaluating classroom learning by the pupils.

It should also be noted here that where involvement and objectives are incorporated in curricula the teacher will have been a participant in the definition and organization of the above competencies.

Constraint or liberation?

The point of view being promulgated on the basis of project experience and study is that any constraint upon teachers involved in the above suggestions is no greater than is required in any other method of achieving a professional consensus within the school about the curriculum for slow learners. In the wider sense of parental and community involvement there is a different kind of constraint, but it is no more than is necessary once it is agreed that the aims and objectives of the education of slow learners *is* of parental and community concern and is a responsibility which is wider than that carried by the teachers. In the best schools this is already accepted and account is taken of the teacher's responsibility to the community in shaping curricula. But the process is often teacher-determined, and informal to such an extent that parents and others are not fully aware of the degree to which schools take account of wider views. By openly inviting and developing the partnership, justice is seen to be done with all the positive effects which that can have on home–school–community relationships. Against this minimum, reasonable constraint must be set the support which the curriculum gives to the teacher through clarity of objectives, and the quality of communication arising not merely through the clarity of curricular documents – important though that is – but through the involvement of the teacher in the partnership process which makes possible the clarity. This clarity and involvement ensure that the teacher in the classroom is as fully prepared as possible for the tasks and decisions resting on the intimacy of knowledge about the situations and potentials of the pupils which must be taken account of in selecting, organizing and presenting learning experiences. The complexity and importance of this task should not be undervalued, for the success of the curriculum depends upon it. Wrong or inappropriate decisions here mean that the anticipated objectives of the curriculum will not become actual achieved objectives. Nor should there be any undervaluing of the sensitivity, insight and warmth which must be combined with rich educational background and professional competence if even the well-prepared teacher is to carry out her demanding tasks with optimum efficiency. In the absence of the kind of preparation and support provided by the involvement–objectives curriculum, the individual teacher must work out for herself all the curricular issues in order to exercise efficiently and appropriately the intimate decisions of the classroom which only she can contend with. Project experience suggests that this situation subjects the teacher to the most serious constraint of all – the constraint of the impossible task – and that its most severe effect is the removal of any sense of direction or purpose from classroom activities. Set against this, the support of the involvement–objectives curriculum can be seen as a *liberation of the teacher*: a liberation, that is, which frees her to work creatively in the critical intimacy of the classrooms. It is one purpose of the curriculum to ensure that the teacher is able to achieve this creativity in her work, and where this purpose is fulfilled, there is no need for the curriculum to pass the classroom door.

Responsibility of the classroom teacher

The above discussion has emphasized the importance of the classroom teacher's involvement with other partners in shaping the aims and terminal objectives of the curriculum, and with professional colleagues in organizing intermediate objectives within the school. Also stressed is the unique responsibility of the classroom teacher for decisions about the pupil's learning which can only be made in the classroom situation, and which demand for their efficiency knowledge which has the quality of intimacy. One disadvantage of this situation is that the essential intimacy is to some extent in opposition to the equally essential objectivity which teachers of slow learners must retain if they are to make proper, professional evaluation of their own work. Central to the stress of working with slow learners is the necessity for the teacher to become totally and absolutely involved with the pupils in the learning situations; but from time to time, the teacher must emerge from this intimacy and warmth and, in the cold light of intellect, objectively view situations, pupils and pupil progress for what they really are. The more successfully the teacher achieves intimacy with pupils, the greater the threat to objectivity – even to the extent of teachers' identifying with pupils in opposition to the views of parents or community in a way which may not always be in the pupils' best interests. There are two safeguards against the danger of loss of objectivity by the classroom teacher. The first is professional and involves the scrutiny of learning experiences by the headteacher and professional advisers of the LEA (Table 8, curricular area 6); the second is the involvement of the other partners in the curriculum in the evaluation of the achieved outcomes of the curriculum (Table 8, curricular area 7). The contention is that classroom teachers should welcome the involvement of professional colleagues and other partners in the evaluation of their work and the outcomes of the school curriculum as a balance for the intimacy and involvement which is an inseparable part of the efficient teaching of slow-learning pupils. There is also the possibility that the techniques, once established, would serve to reduce stress for the teachers. Again, in the better schools, account is taken of wider views in the evaluation of curricula and teaching but, as with the aims, the process is often informal and teacher-dominated to a degree which conceals it from parents and the community. It should be more formalized and more open.

But where is responsibility to reside?

It has been implied that failure to define responsibility for the curriculum is a contributory factor in the current negative attitude in schools, and accounts also for some of the uncertainty expressed by teachers in the project schools. While suggestions such as those made above go some way to resolving tensions between teachers, parents and the community by indicating areas of responsibility and leading roles, they do not of themselves allocate overall responsibility for the curriculum for slow-learning pupils. Yet the need for clear and firm definition of responsibility is one of the major findings of the project study. It is not within the brief of the project to discuss the question of *legal* responsibility, but some suggestions about operational responsibility cannot be avoided.

First, the responsibility itself should be defined. Consistent with the suggestions made above for an involvement–objectives curriculum for slow learners, the overall operational responsibility is not for the detail of the curriculum as such but for the establishment of a permanent and ongoing process in which the partners will produce, evaluate and refine the curricula for slow-learning pupils. The project study suggests that, as the educational system is at present organized, only the local education authority is in a position to discharge that responsibility and in doing so the LEA has three major strengths: its wide representative base in the community, its professional arm of experienced and qualified educational advisers or inspectors, and the community–biased, non-professional communication which can be established through the governors or managers of schools. One necessary comment here is that the professional advisory services of some LEAs will require strengthening by persons qualified and experienced in the education of slow learners. It should be noted that the suggestions imply not only that the LEA must establish and operate the process and machinery which generate curricula for slow learners, but that it must accept responsibility for being the arbiter of quality and must act much more positively in this role. The objective should be a situation in which the professional teachers in the schools, assisted where necessary by the advisory services of the LEA, produce evaluations of their own work for scrutiny by school governors and the LEA, in the process spelling out desirable improvements and developments with clear indications of the resources and support required if these are to be planned advances in the education of slow-learning pupils. It will then be for the LEA to determine necessary priorities between conflicting demands and to phase development in a way compatible with local resources.

The responsibility of the LEA is the major and critical one. The Department of Education and Science may be unable to have any direct effect on the curriculum for slow learners, but it is in a position to overlook general standards and to direct attention to inequalities between different LEAs which affect the concept of equality of educational opportunities for slow learners. Those who train teachers also have a responsibility to discharge. Teachers in training need to be made more aware of the existence and needs of slow learners, and of the developing partnerships which should be involved in the shaping of their education. It would also be helpful if students were made more aware of the intellectual challenge presented by slow learners in order that a fair proportion of intellectually able students are attracted into this area of education.

Developments such as those suggested would make curricular responsibilities clearer and more positive than any which were observed in the project schools. The LEA would have a clear responsibility to maintain a continuous process of curriculum development in the schools; to ensure adequate input to it from parents and from the community; to maintain a professional advisory service which would support the schools and advise on the quality of the curriculum for slow learners; and to provide the facilities and conditions which would enable the schools to provide appropriate and efficient curriculum and teaching for slow-learning pupils. The headteachers and teachers in the schools would be responsible for generating curricula related to the needs of the slow learners in the schools; for making use of parental and community experience in discharging that task; for evaluating the curriculum and maintaining its quality and relevance to the needs of the pupils; and for proper use of the advisory service in discharging curricular responsibilities within the system operated in the LEA

What of the common curriculum?

In proposing a curricular process which leaves the curriculum for slow learners as a local responsibility, the question of the possibility of a common curriculum is also left for local determination. To do otherwise would be a basic contradiction of the principles of the proposal. Yet the question is important and there are aspects of the project study which bear upon it.

The first point to be noted is taken from the discussion of curricular aims. Aims are concerned with the values and principles which should inform the whole of the curricular process. They are ethical and philosophical concepts, and taken together have something about them which indicates what it is to be human and to enjoy one's humanity in interaction with others. That is, they see individuality as requiring a social setting for fulfilment of its richness. In a democratic society, therefore, the aims of education should be universal, applying to all, and indeed any aims which are not applicable to all should be immediately suspect. It is agreed that this amounts to saying that there are no special aims of education which apply exclusively to slow-learning pupils. So here is the start of the common curriculum in the commonality of the aim of education.

In the discussion of objectives it was stressed that objectives should be behavioural; that is, observable in the behaviour of pupils who had achieved them. It was also stressed that they should be, among other things, realistic; that is, capable of being achieved by the pupils for whom they were proposed given a degree of effort on their part appropriate to the pupils' approximate potential and stage of development. Put another way, objectives are determined in a psychological, sociological frame of reference which is different from the frame of reference in which aims are defined. By their very nature objectives *must* take account of the individual, his propensities and his total life situation. The principle of realism not only allows but demands that objectives should vary in order to be consistent with the different potential and patterns of potential in individuals. Yet these different objectives have a common element: all are calculated to ensure that different individuals achieve the common aims of education as richly and as fully as individuality allows. And one common objective of education is the stimulation and pursuit of maximum possible personal richness for every individual.

Another feature of the discussion takes this argument further and suggests that even where there is wide difference in the intellectual potential of individual pupils, this need not necessarily require different objectives in the curriculum. This is the implication of the earlier discussion of 'levels' for the achievement of objectives. It will be recalled, from the review of literature (Chapter III), that the levels involved *understanding* or *awareness* for knowledge and *mastery* or *familiarity* for skills. No doubt these levels for achievement can and should be refined further, but even in their present crude state they offer not only the reality of common aims but the matching of these by the maximum of common objectives.

Another contribution to a common curriculum is the realization that different objectives for individuals of different potential can, in practice, embrace common curriculum content and involve common learning experiences. It is the behavioural outcomes that are specified which will reflect the individual differences, and over wide areas only the teacher need be aware of these.

It was a wise man who once observed that we all must of necessity be citizens but it was not necessary that we should all be plumbers. One could add: or philosophers, scientists, mathematicians, etc., and even add further that whichever of these we are we are very strange individuals if we are any of these for the whole of our time. In sociological terms this means that individuals have many roles and these are reflected in membership of many sub-groups. Though in our society status and role interact and overlap, there is the possibility of analysis to determine both common roles and common elements in different roles, which may identify areas suitable for exploitation in common curricula. Here is a possible contribution to a common curriculum which deserves investigation.

A development of the above theme would be more serious study of the physical, cultural, social and economic differences between and within human societies, using more freely techniques and results from the social sciences. The objective would be to extend pupils' understanding of what it is to be a member of the human race, in the process reducing the primitive fear of difference and replacing it by an acknowledgement of difference as a human strength.

And what of exploiting historical studies to achieve understanding of the idea of development in the societies and affairs of men; or of geography to foster concepts of man's relationship to his environment (which often explains differences) and man's interaction for mutual benefit (which often negates differences)? Is it impossible for such studies to be pursued at different levels for common benefit as another contribution to a common curriculum?

The graphic arts, crafts and music offer opportunity for studies at sensory and aesthetic levels accessible for most students, and have the advantage of reducing the reliance on language. Properly handled, these curricular areas can become the basis of common experience for pupils of a wide range of ability. Theatre, films, television and radio also offer the possibility of shared experiences for pupils who could not share written literature because of wide differences in reading levels. Are these possibilities being fully exploited for contributions to a common curriculum?

Language itself offers possibility of contribution to a common curriculum. It is involved in some of the later suggestions in the previous paragraph, but it also needs to be considered from the point of registers, or the use of language appropriate to situation. It may not be possible for the language of the slow learner to attain some of the registers of his more intellectual peers, but there is something wrong in a democratic society if intelligent members cannot communicate with the less intelligent in situations and about topics which are common to both groups. Has this dichotomy yet disappeared? And if not, might this be a further contribution to a common curriculum?

Mathematics and science are difficult curricular areas, and the project study has shown that they are not well covered with slow learners. Yet it cannot be denied that everyday concepts of measurement, of calculation, of growth, shape, symmetry, conservation, graphic communication, etc., must be established at a minimum level for slow learners. Similarly with science. How can slow learners understand their society if they do not have some concepts of objectivity of evidence, of data relating to problems and shaping solutions, of what it means to be intellectually honest? And surely they must be made aware of the contribution of science to the welfare of man and the shape of western society? The neglect of science in the education of slow learners is especially tragic, as the basic procedures of science, with their emphasis on concrete experiment and sensory evidence, have much in common with the modes of learning known to be necessary with slow-learning pupils. It should be possible to devise a common-core science curriculum which slow learners could share with more able pupils, even if the level of objectives differed between the groups. Perhaps teachers of slow learners should give a positive lead here.

Physical education and movement have always contributed to common curricula. What is required here is more serious attention to the quality of work with slow learners, particularly on the lines suggested by Bantock as indicated in the review of literature (Chapter III).

Finally, there is the religious and moral element of a common curriculum. The outlines of Christianity and the Bible story have a cultural value quite distinct from personal religious belief, and slow learners need at least an awareness of these, and of minority religious views and practices with which they may have contact, just as minority slow learners should be aware of the Christian ethic and practice. This is the heart of common curricula in concepts and beliefs which, though superficially different, have a common content reflecting a deep human need that has leapt the obstacles of time, space and culture in the family of man.

It may be asked why there has been so much emphasis on a common curriculum. There are four main reasons. First, there is the fundamental nature of the questions as posed in the review of literature. Secondly, the absence of the concept noted in the curricular documents and in the discussions with teachers of slow learners in the project schools. Thirdly, the only common curricula observed were in mixed-ability schools where there was a thoughtless and inevitable assumption that slow learners should follow the normal curriculum. Fourthly, there is the comment of Hirst on the common curriculum, that there are 'no adequate grounds for saying this is impossible when we have in fact spent so little of our effort in trying to achieve this'.[5] Perhaps the time has come to increase our efforts in this direction.

References

1. W. K. BRENNAN, *Shaping the Education of Slow Learners*. Routledge & Kegan Paul, 1974. 'The curricular needs of slow-learning pupils', in Report of International Conference, Canterbury. National Council for Special Education, 1975, pp. 245–59. 'The curricular needs of slow-learning children', in A. F. Laing (ed.), *Trends in the Education of Children with Special Learning Needs*. Faculty of Education, University College of Swansea, 1975, pp. 23–32. *Reading for Slow Learners: a Curriculum Guide*. Schools Council Curriculum Bulletin 7. Evans/Methuen Educational, 1978, chapter V.
2. Inner London Education Authority Television Service, *Teaching the Slow Learner*, a series of ten videotapes made in the project schools with W. K. Brennan acting as consultant. (On sale or for hire from Guild Sound and Vision, Woodston House Oundle Road, Peterborough, PE2 9PZ.)
3. K. WEDELL, *Learning and Perceptuo-motor Disabilities in Children*. John Wiley, New York, 1974.
4. R. GULLIFORD, *Special Educational Needs*. Routledge & Kegan Paul, 1971, pp. 67–8.
5. P. H. HIRST, 'The logic of the curriculum', *Journal of Curriculum Studies*, 1, 1969, 142–58. Reprinted in R. Hooper (ed.), *The Curriculum*. Oliver & Boyd, Edinburgh, 1971, pp. 232–50.

Project team and consultative committee

Project team

Director
W. K. Brennan

Research associates
C. R. Cooper
Miss A. Richards

Secretaries
Mrs A. Rees (until June 1974)
Mrs M. Dann (from June 1974)

School visitors

Mrs K. F. Devereux	Tutor, Special Education Courses, Cambridge Institute of Education
R. Ablewhite	Formerly tutor, Special Education Courses City of Leicester College of Education

Consultative committee

Mrs K. F. Devereux (Chairman)	Tutor, Special Education Courses, Cambridge Institute of Education
R. B. Barnes	Headmaster, Great Stony Residential Special School (ESN), ILEA
Mrs M. Bright-Thomas	Headteacher, Orchard Infants School, ILEA
J. H. Broom	Headmaster, Coed Eva Junior School, Gwent
R. Bushell	Advisory Officer, Head of Remedial Service, Staffordshire
N. L. Dodsworth	Headmaster, Bramcote Hills Secondary School, Nottingham

Mrs F. C. A. Lee Cave	Great Dunmow C of E Primary School, Essex
Mrs L. A. C. Marigold	Formerly Head of Remedial Department, Woodberry Down Comprehensive School, London N4
†L. J. McDonald	Formerly Headmaster, Stanley Special School (ESN), Liverpool
J. W. D. Thomas	Remedial and Home Teaching Adviser, Glamorgan
S. J. Tunstall	Headmaster, Longford Day Special School (ESN), Gloucester
A. A. Williams	Tutor, Special Education Courses, Kingston-upon-Hull College of Education